Verena Kley

The Taxation of Capitalistic Beq

GABLER RESEARCH

Verena Kley

The Taxation of Capitalistic Bequests

GABLER

RESEARCH

Bibliographic information published by the Deutsche Nationalbibliothek
The Deutsche Nationalbibliothek lists this publication in the Deutsche Nationalbibliografie; detailed bibliographic data are available in the Internet at http://dnb.d-nb.de.

Doctoral thesis accepted by the Department of Economics and Business Engineering at Karlsruhe Institute of Technology (KIT) – University of the State Baden-Wuerttemberg and National Center of the Helmholtz Association.

Date of oral examination: June 30, 2011

Supervisor: Professor Dr. Berthold U. Wigger
Second advisor: Professor Dr. Ingrid Ott

1st Edition 2012

All rights reserved
© Gabler Verlag | Springer Fachmedien Wiesbaden GmbH 2012

Editorial Office: Marta Grabowski | Anita Wilke

Gabler Verlag is a brand of Springer Fachmedien.
Springer Fachmedien is part of Springer Science+Business Media.
www.gabler.de

No part of this publication may be reproduced, stored in a retrieval system or transmitted, in any form or by any means, electronic, mechanical, photocopying, recording, or otherwise, without the prior written permission of the copyright holder.

Registered and/or industrial names, trade names, trade descriptions etc. cited in this publication are part of the law for trade-mark protection and may not be used free in any form or by any means even if this is not specifically marked.

Cover design: KünkelLopka Medienentwicklung, Heidelberg
Printed on acid-free paper
Printed in Germany

ISBN 978-3-8349-3374-4

Acknowledgement

This thesis would not have been possible without the help and guidance of the following people. It is them that I owe my deepest gratitude.

Professor Dr. Berthold U. Wigger, my supervisor, who supported my efforts from the initial to the final level and who gave me the necessary freedom for my research project. My second advisor, Professor Dr. Ingrid Ott, for her constructive comments, as well as Professor Dr. Siegfried Berninghaus and Professor Dr. Stefan Tai as members of the examination board.

I would like to thank my colleagues, who accompanied me the last three and a half years in Nuremberg as well as in Karlsruhe and who participated in this research project with interest and enthusiasm. My special thanks go to Christiane Lorenz und Lisa Tillmann for inspiring discussions and mental support despite being in crucial stages of their own dissertations.

I would also like to thank in particular my entire family. My parents, Carola and Otto Kley, who have always supported, encouraged and believed in me. My brother, Fabian Kley, for all his encouragement and helpful advice. And last but not least, Tobias Patzelt for his love, support and constant patience during the final stages of this dissertation.

Verena Kley

Contents

List of Tables

List of Figures

List of Symbols

LATIN SYMBOLS:

a	wealth threshold for capitalistic preferences (modified Stone-Geary parameter)
A	descendant's attention
b	private bequest
c	private consumption
d^f	minimum capital stock required to install a foundation
e	gross labor income
E^b	inheritance tax effect on future inheritances
E^l	inheritance tax effect on labor income
f	government spending per capita
$F(\cdot)$	children's preference distribution under a fixed budget
g	government budget per capita
G^*	optimal non-linear tax system
$G(\cdot)$	distribution of initial ability
$h(\cdot)$	utility
H	high income individual
$H(\cdot)$	initial wealth distribution
i	individuals
I	inheritance
k^f	proportional costs required to run a foundation
l	time used for labor
L	low income individual
m	number of parents
M	median voter
n	rate of population growth
o	old individual
p^A	price for descendant's attention
p_L, p_H	earning abilities of high and low type individuals
q_L, q_H	social planner weights given to high and low type individuals

r	interest rate
r_f	rate of return of a foundation
s	private savings
$S(\cdot)$	children's preference distribution under a fixed labor income tax
t	period indicator
T	transfers during lifetime
$u(\cdot)$	utility
$U(\cdot)$	lifetime utility
$v(\cdot)$	indirect utility
w	wealth holding
$\bar{w}$	wealth level in the social environment
$\widetilde{w}$	wealth level at which consumers begin to bequeath
$\hat{w}$	wealth level at which consumers begin to install a foundation
x	net labor income
y	young individual
z	political weight of an individual

GREEK SYMBOLS:

α	social rate of discounting the welfare of future generations
β	rate of altruism
χ	degree of homogeneity within a pressure group
ε	intensity of weighting paternalistic bequests
ε	voting costs
η	number of pressure group members
ϕ	relative risk aversion of wealth
γ	intensity of capitalist spirit
λ	Lagrange multiplier
τ^b	tax on bequests
τ^l	tax on labor earnings
τ^r	tax on capital earnings
μ	relative risk aversion of consumption
$\nu(\cdot)$	utility
θ	survival probability
σ	time preference rate
ψ	social status
ξ	interest rate for intra-family credits

1 Introduction

1.1 Problem definition

A tax on bequests, like any tax on personal wealth, is fundamentally motivated by the aim to counterbalance wealth inequality in society.[1] The question thereby arises, whether bequests to future generations contribute to society's wealth distribution, and hence are justified being taxed, or whether the inequality in wealth can solely be attributed to the inequality in earnings. In Germany, for example, it can be observed that the wealthiest 10% of the population receive 25% of the total income. However, indicating a significant difference in saving behavior, they possess a substantially even higher percentage of almost 60% of the entire national economy's wealth.[2] This distribution is similar in almost all industrialized countries.[3] Recent work has therefore focused on intergenerational wealth transfers, implying widespread agreement that these transfers account for a significant fraction of household wealth. The quantitative estimates, however, vary widely: Kotlikoff and Summers (1981) conclude that roughly 50 to 80 percent of total wealth is generated by gifts and bequests, whereas Aaron and Munnell (1992) or Gale and Scholz (1994) estimate this figure between 25 and 50 percent.

Anticipating that intergenerational wealth transfers convey benefits above the recipients' abilities, the taxation of bequests hence can contribute to achieve equality of opportunities by redistributing wealth within society. Thereby, it mainly affects those individuals who transfer considerable amounts of wealth to future generations.

Thus, as a result, a taxation of wealth transfers, on the one hand, is able to balance the unequal distribution of economic, social or political power. On the other hand, it is considered as a form of double taxation, which undermines the incen-

[1] Whereas in some nations the testator is levied by wealth transfer taxes directly, in others it is the recipient who is charged. Normally, the former is levied by an *estate tax*, whereas the latter pays an *inheritance tax*. However, this distinction is not always respected. For example, the 'inheritance tax' in the UK is a tax on personal representatives, and is therefore, strictly speaking, an estate tax. Both terms are used interchangeably for bequest and wealth transfer taxation in the theoretical analysis of this study. A detailed differentiation is given in Chapter 5.

[2] See Frick et al. (2007).

[3] See e.g. Hindricks (2004) observing data for the United States.

tive to save, impedes the continuation of family-owned businesses and welcomes strategic tax planning.[4]

The redistributive character of wealth transfer taxation suggests that the more concentrated society's wealth, the more likely and the more intense bequest taxes are. However, it can be observed that almost all developed countries rely extensively on progressive personal income taxation, whereas none derives significant revenue from the taxation of wealth transfers.[5]

Table 1.1: Wealth transfer tax vs. income tax revenues of selected OECD countries in 2007

Share of total revenues generated by ... (in %)	DE	ES	FR	GB	IT	SE	US
bequest taxation	0.48	0.73	1.08	0.77	0.02	0	0.81
income taxation	31.21	33.37	23.86	39.51	33.73	38.74	49.02

Source: Revenue Statistics 1965 - 2007 OECD (2009); own calculations.[6]

Instead of a moderate taxation of all wealth transfers, most OECD countries have resorted to high tax rates levied solely on large bequests. Due to high exemption levels, the larger part of the population is able to transfer wealth to future generations free of taxes, whereas a minority of rich individuals is fully affected by excessive taxation which they naturally seek to avoid. As an outcome, tax revenues are negligibly low, inducing that the taxation of bequests has long been and still is subject to extensive discussion, with supporters demanding much higher taxation and opponents calling for its abolition. At the same time, the economic analysis of an *optimal* bequest tax design arouses growing political interest.

In general, current systems of taxing wealth transfers have been subject to significant and increasing criticism, and deliberations on bequest tax reforms are observable in many industrialized countries.[7] The discussion is basically triggered

[4]See Gale and Slemrod (2000) or Donges et al. (2007).

[5]See OECD (2009) or Aaron and Munnell (1992).

[6]Country names are abbreviated according to two-letter code elements of the International Organization of Standardization (ISO).

[7]A brief outlook: In the US, estate taxes were given a "one year repeal" in 2010 (effectuated by a temporary tax rate of 0%) in order to reintroduce an estate tax, scheduled with higher top rates and reduced exemption amounts, in 2011. In December 2010, President Barack Obama, however, has signed legislation that exempts estates smaller than 5 million US-dollars from the federal estate

by the polarizing nature of bequest taxation, arising on the death of an individual and levying the total value of money and property of the deceased.

However, wealth taxes applied to enhance redistribution appear to fail their main objective. Empirical data reveals that wealth inequality in many OECD countries is increasing, implying that the gap between rich and poor is widening. On top of the wealthy households this process is also induced by a shrinking middle class.[8] Considering a huge share of personal wealth is generated by gifts and bequests, inequality is passed on and even intensified from generation to generation. Thereby, the question arises as to how the taxation of intergenerational wealth transfers can be improved to counter this development in the future.

Covering one of the most widely discussed tax instruments in fiscal policy this thesis therefore aims to answer *"How to optimally tax capitalistic bequests?"* by examining the application of wealth transfer taxes on very rich individuals.[9]

1.2 A note on optimal tax theory

To be able to answer the core-question of this study it is necessary to define which attributes must be fulfilled for reaching optimal taxation. Thus, in order to judge any good tax system, appropriate criteria is needed, and optimal tax design is generally measured against three key figures:

- the degree of efficiency it generates,
- the administrative costs it produces and
- the political constraints it faces.

Whereas the first quantifies undesired distortions on individual decisions to work as well as to accumulate and dispose wealth, the second measures government expenditures for both assessment and collection of taxes. The third attribute, finally, depicts political consequences when implementing or reforming a tax system, which inevitably creates winners and losers.

---

tax, and creates a maximum estate tax rate lower than that in 2009. Contrasting, Sweden, Portugal, and Austria abolished their inheritance tax in recent years. In France, Great Britain as well as in Germany inheritance taxes are subject to constant changes in which all recently extended tax exemption levels. See Chapter 5.

[8] See OECD (2008).

[9] Throughout this study, wealth transfer taxation solely focuses on those transfers occurring at death, entirely neglecting inter-vivos gifts, which are taxed in accordance to bequests in almost all industrialized countries.

Hence, in order to find the optimal tax system, literature on tax theory deals with these criteria by providing normative as well as positive implications. Though, analyzing government activities from different angles, both approaches aspire to optimize and to explain government decisions on public expenditures and revenues. Therein, literature on optimal taxation typically treats the social planner as a utilitarian, using a social welfare function that is determined by the utilities of individuals in society.

Based on welfare economics, *normative* tax theory originates in a major early contribution of Ramsey (1927), upon which the work of Mirrlees (1971) is established. Ramsey (1927) showed that a social planner, raising a given amount of tax revenue through taxes on commodities only, should impose these taxes in inverse proportion to the representative consumer's elasticity of demand for the good. So that commodities which experience inelastic demand are taxed more heavily. Ramsey's efforts have had a profound impact on tax theory as well as other fields such as public goods pricing and regulation. Mirrlees (1971) launched the second wave of optimal tax models by suggesting a way of formalizing the government's problem that deals explicitly with unobserved heterogeneity among taxpayers. Thereby, the Mirrlees approach formalizes the classic trade-off between equality and efficiency that governments face, and it has become the dominant approach for tax theorists. The optimal tax problem turns into a game of imperfect information between taxpayers and the social planner, who strives to tax those of high ability and give transfers to those of low ability. Therefore, the social planner needs to make sure that the tax system does not induce those of high ability to pretend being of low ability.[10] Generally, the aim of normative tax theory is to provide ideal tax policies which minimize welfare losses and hence maximize society's welfare in a given analytical framework.[11]

Positive tax theory, going back to early representatives like Wicksell (1896) and Lindahl (1919) and more recently to Buchanan (1976), Brennan and Buchanan (1977), as well as Hettich and Winer (1984), however, considers optimal tax policies as equilibrium outcomes of a collective choice process with self-interested political agents. Thus the optimal tax design is constrained by political as well as economic forces which are shaped by individual tax preferences, generating

[10] Indeed, modern Mirrleesian analysis often relies on the "revelation principle". According to this classic game theoretic result, any optimal allocation of resources can be achieved through a policy under which individuals voluntarily reveal their types in response to the incentives provided.

[11] While the optimal taxation literature is large and complex, there are several reviews of the material. Auerbach (1985), Stern (1974), and Stiglitz (1987) offer technical summaries of optimal commodity and income taxation, whereas Slemrod (1990) presents a critical review of the modern optimal tax literature.

an incentive for redistribution between majority and minority fiscal interests. Tax policy thereby is endogenously defined by the voters.

Regarding the discussion of optimal bequest taxation, existing literature mainly concentrates on normative aspects, analyzing distributive as well as allocative effects of wealth transfer taxation. Therein, the implications critically depend upon the type of bequest motive one assumes. These are divided in several distinct categories, ranging from unplanned bequests to personal motivations. Following Davies (1981), the former result from uncertainty concerning length of lifetime coupled with restrictions on the availability of annuity insurance contracts, whereas the latter can be further subdivided into three common bequest motives. According to Barro (1974) and Becker (1974) individuals have altruistic preferences, caring about the heir's utility. Another motive, evolved by Blinder (1976) or Andreoni (1989), assumes individuals to care directly about the amount of wealth transferred to the descendants. A third is based on Bernheim, Shleifer and Summers (1985) or Kotlikoff and Spivak (1981), depicting wealth transfers as payments associated with services transacted within families. While unplanned bequests shift the tax burden completely towards the heir, planned bequests at least partly incorporate the tax burden of future generations.

1.3 Aim and structure of this study

To answer the central question of this thesis, a theoretical analysis is employed. Therein, the specific properties of optimal normative as well as positive wealth transfer taxation focusing on very wealthy individuals are derived, in order to finally give recommendations for bequest tax design. In doing so, this study aims to answer the following question:

1. Up to which extent should wealth transfers of the very rich be optimally taxed within a society characterized by heterogeneity according to age and wealth?
2. Which tax rates on wealth transfers of the very wealthy are politically viable – obtaining the majority of votes – within such a heterogeneous society?
3. How can current bequest tax policy be assessed, by application of the aforementioned findings?

Thus, when wanting to analyze optimal bequest tax design, it is of major interest to have a closer look at wealthy individuals as they ultimately pay wealth transfer taxes at exceedingly high rates.

In order to identify any rich society member, a characterization by Atkinson (1981) can be used, implying that individuals whose wealth holding would enable an entire life of leisure are considered as 'very wealthy'. Thus, the critical wealth level to separate a rich from a less wealthy individual can be determined by the sum of the individual's life cycle incomes.[12]

It can be observed that the behavior of the very wealthy often differs from the rest of society.[13] De Nardi (2004), for example, shows that rich individuals often continue working, even though having accumulated enough wealth to live in extreme luxury until life's end, and that they further leave most of their wealth to charity rather than to their children. The question thereby arises, whether this is due to the fact that, being a scaled-up version of everybody else, they save and bequeath more in absolute terms only, or whether rich individual's preferences to accumulate and dispose wealth differs from those exhibited by any other citizen. In the latter case it can be asked whether behavioral responses emerge under the influence of wealth transfer taxation, and whether wealthy individuals are able to generate political influence.

Generally, a wealth creating ambition, continuing even beyond death, is attributed to most rich individuals. Describing an innate desire to accumulate wealth throughout lifetime, this ambition is known as **'capitalist spirit'** – a notion that has been shaped by Weber (1905, p.53)

> Man is dominated by the making of money, by acquisition as the ultimate purpose of life.

More recent findings suggest, due to 'capitalist spirit' wealthy individuals either derive utility from terminal wealth, applied by Zou (1994), Carroll (1998), and Francis (2008)), or gain utility by a 'desire of immortality', which is argued by Davies and Shorrocks (2000) and Luo and Young (2009).

Whilst the analysis of universal bequest motives has been widely explored in tax literature, the specific characteristics of wealthy individuals have mostly been neglected. Even though empirical work, like Arrondel and Laferrère (2001), De Nardi (2004), or Dynan, Skinner and Zeldes (2004), reveals that the upper tail of the wealth distribution exhibits different patterns of saving, this phenomenon has received little attention in theoretical literature. These particularities, however, seem decisive for optimal tax policy design.

[12] For further motivation see Arrondel and Laferrère (2001). According to them the wealthiest 2% in society can be regarded as 'very wealthy'.

[13] See Arrondel and Laferrère (2001) or Dynan, Skinner and Zeldes (2004).

This study, therefore, reviews the optimal wealth transfer taxation with particular attention to very wealthy individuals, enriching the current debates on bequest tax reforms and giving recommendations for political decision makers.

The thesis is subdivided into six chapters, outlined in the following. The overall structure additionally is visualized in Figure 1.1.

In the following, **Chapter 2** analyzes the implications for optimal bequest tax design, compiling existing literature on intergenerational wealth transfers. Recommendation for the optimal taxation of these transfers is given, with regard to the specific attributes of the most common bequest motives. Current state of scientific knowledge apparently implies the optimal solution neither to be constituted by radical bequest tax abolition nor by confiscatory taxation.[14] Normative theory rather suggests a moderate taxation, adjusted to the underlying bequest motive, which thereby maximizes society's welfare and simultaneously minimizes behavioral responses of testators and heirs. Literature focusing on the positive analysis of bequest taxation, on the contrary, recommends wealth transfers to be taxed at higher rates than normatively optimal, in order to generate political majorities.

On the basis of these findings, the following chapters are then dedicated to the wealth accumulation of the very rich, incorporating the idea of the *'capitalist spirit'*. A normative as well as positive analysis of the optimal wealth transfer taxation of the very rich is developed under the assumption that individuals, when becoming wealthier, rather dedicate utility to the immortality of own lifework and property than to family concerns.

Chapter 3 analyzes the normative aspects of taxing wealth transfers of the very wealthy. A comparison of existing universal bequest motives to the saving behavior of the very rich indicates that their motivation to bequeath does not appear to follow family concerns and that their fortunes are often inherited to own foundations rather than to their descendants. In order to analyze rich individuals' preferences and the impact of a bequest tax on their behavior as well as on social welfare, a 'model of overlapping generations' is introduced.[15] Observing the distortive and redistributive effects for individual as well as for social welfare, it can be shown that with increasing wealth inequality a wealth transfer taxation of the very rich may contribute to society's welfare.

Chapter 4 models a positive equilibrium, deriving the political-economic implications for optimal bequest taxation of capitalistic individuals. Again, an OLG model is used to determine the politically optimal level of wealth transfer taxation, incorporating a median-voter approach with agents being heterogeneous accord-

[14] See Cremer and Pestieau (2006), or Gale and Perozek (2000).

[15] In the following, the abbreviated term 'OLG model' is used in accordance with the scientific literature.

ing to age and wealth. Bearing in mind that the number of individuals affected by bequest taxation is rather small, one could expect tax rates on wealth transfers to be even confiscatory, since a winning coalition of society's poorest fifty percent could theoretically enhance their members' welfare by redistributing wealth to the mean. Using numerical simulation, individual tax preferences are analyzed with and without redistributive public pension payments, showing that age composition as well as wealth distribution in society crucially determines tax policy.

Chapter 5 explores the interplay between tax theory and tax policy, comparing the theoretical findings with current tax policy in selected OECD countries. Special attention is paid to German inheritance tax.

Finally, **Chapter 6** summarizes the major results of this study and provides policy recommendations for future wealth transfer taxation.

Figure 1.1: Structure of the thesis

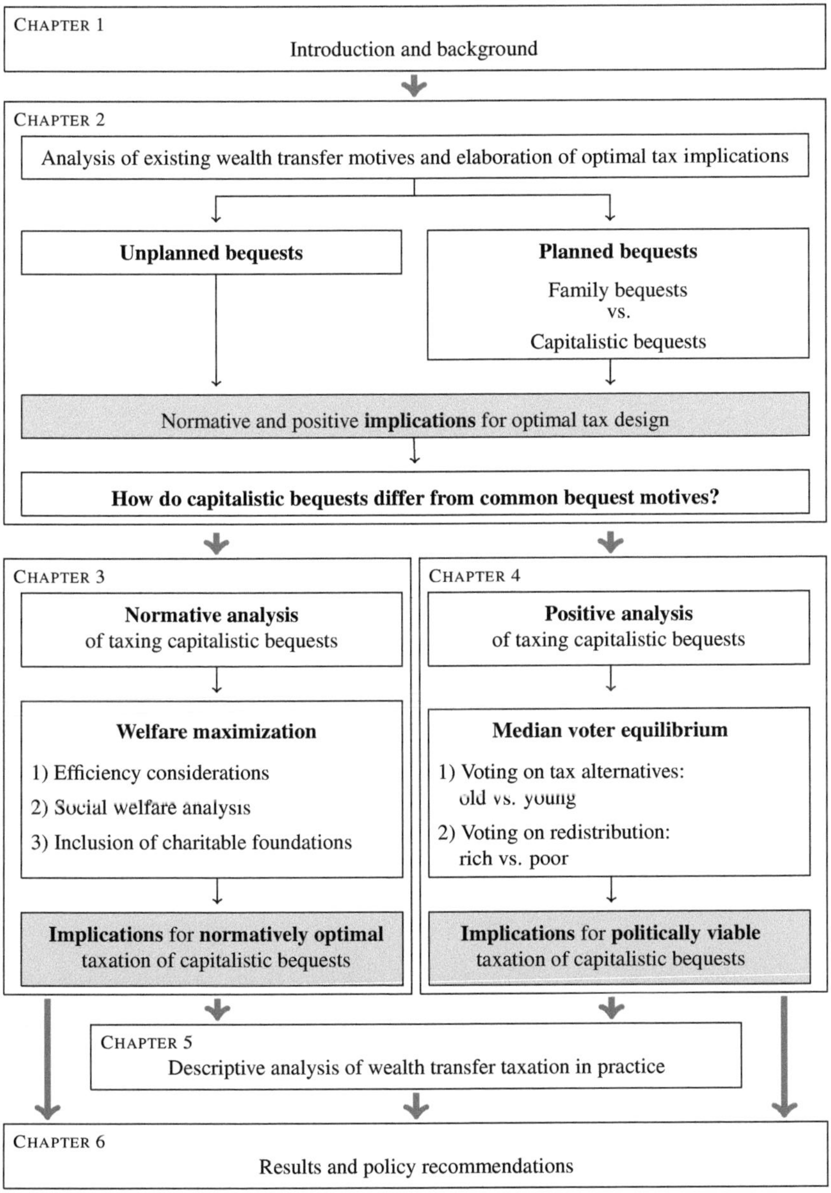

2 Optimal wealth transfer taxation: a review of existing literature

"The art of taxation consists in so plucking the goose as to obtain the largest amount of feathers with the least possible amount of hissing."

Jean B. Colbert

The economics of taxation have been a major subject of analysis throughout history, and it is not difficult to understand the source of this widespread interest. Taxes directly affect the daily lives of individuals, while also providing revenues of the state. They give the government access to private economic resources and enable the provision of public services. Their imposition, however, influences the distribution of personal income and may alter the division of wealth among citizens.

The economic analysis of wealth transfer taxation is essentially based on the underlying assumptions on individual bequest motives. A universal recommendation for optimal tax design, therefore, is barely feasible, since the attributes of each motive differ completely. Thus, in order to evaluate existing tax systems and give policy advice it is inevitable to derive differentiated implications for each of the common theories on bequests motives in literature.

From a *normative* perspective, it can be shown that those bequests aimed to directly benefit the heirs are more sensitive to taxation than those transferred in order to either receive services in return or to generate utility by giving per se. Thus, classifying the different intentions, one can argue that wealth transfers to own descendants might be much more dynastically motivated than those to distant relatives.

As soon as *political* considerations are regarded, irrespective of the various bequest motives, literature implies the imposition of higher tax rates than normatively optimal, in order to generate political majorities. Arguing that the unaffected can outnumber the affected, this might by the reason why many countries extensively tax at least large wealth transfers.

In order to analyze these aspects, Section 2.1 gives an overview of the most common bequest motives in literature, explaining their specific attributes by using an overlapping generation setting. Based on these findings, Section 2.2 collates normative aspects of bequest taxation and gives implications on how to optimally tax each bequest motive in order to maximize society's welfare. Section 2.3 outlines the aspects of positive wealth transfer tax analysis within majoritarian voting processes. Finally, Section 2.4 compares normative and positive tax theory results and concludes.

2.1 Motives for intergenerational wealth transfers

Within studies on national saving behavior in the early 1930s, already two fundamental bequest motives had been developed. It was observed that capital accumulation often causes large shares of these savings to be inherited.[16] Thus, on the one hand, they identified a capitalistic saving motive that was attributed solely to the wealthy strata of the population, in which wealth is utilized to acquire prestige, power and control. Savings of the financially weak individuals, on the other hand, were revealed solely to serve for funding retirement. Hence, these individuals were supposed to gradually dissave assets until death. While bequests among the former are considered to be mainly strategic, inheritances among the latter are, if occurring at all, mainly accidental and thereby unplanned.

In the late 1970s, studies on family economics renewed these class-based considerations. Further transfer motives were identified, among which two motives received particular awareness in literature – one being pure altruism, based upon research of Barro (1974) and Becker and Tomes (1979), the other being an exchange motive nurtured by self-interest, constituted by Bernheim, Shleifer and Summers (1985).

The motivation to transfer wealth to future generations can thus be divided into several distinct categories, which can be further aggregated into three main groups:

- *Unplanned bequests* are not induced by the wish to bequeath wealth. They rather result from capital market imperfections and uncertainty concerning the length of own lifetime. Hence, wealth can neither be invested optimally nor consumed completely.

- *Planned*, family-oriented bequests follow a progeny-focused interest. They range from altruistic care about children's wellbeing to strategic payments associated with services transacted within families.

[16]For a historical survey see Modigliani (1988).

- *Capitalistic bequests* are a specification of planned transfers, but solely a phenomenon of very wealthy individuals. The motive to transfer wealth to future generations pursues the idea of guaranteeing the survival of own lifework even beyond death, in form of a foundation, a family trust, or a company dynasty.

In order to present the specific characteristics of each of these bequest motives in more detail, I introduce a model of overlapping generations. Therefore, I consider identical individuals to live for two periods each, consuming in both but working only in the first. Each individual receives an exogenous labor income e as well as an inheritance I in the first period of life.[17] Therewith, she funds private consumption c_t and c_{t+1} when young and old, respectively, and transfers the residual as bequest b to her descendant. Hence, the individual born in period t, maximizes her lifetime utility by

$$\max U_t = u(c_t, c_{t+1}, b_t), \tag{2.1}$$

subject to the budget constraint

$$e_t + I_t = c_t + \frac{c_{t+1} + b_t}{1+r}, \tag{2.2}$$

with r denoting saving's interest rate. It holds $\partial u(\cdot)/\partial c > 0$ and $\partial u'(\cdot)/\partial c < 0$ as well as $\partial u(\cdot)/\partial b \geq 0$ and $\partial u'(\cdot)/\partial b \leq 0$.

Since the characteristics of each bequest motive can be reflected in the utility function, these are explicitly analyzed in the following.[18]

2.1.1 Unplanned bequests

Although some individuals may not pursue any specific wealth transfer motive, different reasons cause them to be unable to consume their entire savings until the end of life and thus to unintentionally transfer wealth to following generations.

According to Davies (1981) such bequests result from restrictions on the availability of annuity insurance contracts. These induce that individuals neither can nor want to invest their wealth holdings in order to receive regular pension payments. Due to capital market imperfections, they fear uninsurable risks of aging

[17] For sake of simplicity labor earnings e are assumed to be independent from work effort. For the present analysis of bequest motives this assumption does not change the results.

[18] In order to solely focus on wealth transfers made from generation t to $t+1$, I abstract from any inheritances received by the testator I_t as well as from own bequests made by the descendants b_{t+1}.

and instead prepare for unexpected expenditures by undertaking precautionary savings. Naturally, risk aversion leads to excessively high savings, such that sudden death results in unplanned bequests.

Based upon findings of Yaari (1965) and Barro and Friedman (1977), Abel (1985) further observes that precautionary savings and hence unplanned bequests are intensified by incorporating uncertainty about the length of lifetime. If individuals would solely adjust savings to the expected average lifetime, any assets would be spent as soon as exceeding this age. Hence, in order to avoid this situation, risk-averse individuals often save more than necessary. Unplanned bequests, therefore, are not only a side-effect of early death but rather driven by precautionary savings of individuals at any age.

Thus, parent's lifetime utility is determined merely by own consumption. Uncertainty can be illustrated by incorporating a survival probability $0 \leq \theta \leq 1$. It is assumed that all individuals live in the first period with certainty, whilst the probability to survive in the second period is insecure. Hence, an individual born in period t maximizes

$$\max U_t = u(c_t) + \theta u(c_{t+1}),$$

under the budget constraints

$$\begin{aligned} c_t &= e_t - s_t, \\ c_{t+1} &= s_t(1+r). \end{aligned}$$

with s_t denoting savings in period t for consumption in $t+1$. The first order condition then holds

$$\frac{\partial u}{\partial c_t} = \theta \frac{\partial u}{\partial c_{t+1}}(1+r).$$

Let, for the sake of simplicity, $r = 0$. Hence, it can be observed that parents, living the first period only ($\theta = 0$), consume their entire earnings, whilst saving nothing. However, if individuals live until the end of the second period with certainty ($\theta = 1$), they consume one half of their income in t while the other is saved for consumption in $t+1$. In between these extrema, exact wealth planning cannot be accomplished, which inevitably leads to precautionary savings and consequently to unplanned bequests.

Yaari (1965) shows that precautionary savings rise with the survival probability, since the risk to require funding when old increases.[19] It holds that, the earlier the death of individuals with high life expectancy the larger their bequests.[20]

2.1.2 Planned bequests

Bequest motives describing planned, family-concerned wealth transfers can be distinguished into four categories: altruism, retrospective, paternalism, and strategic exchange. Therein, pure altruism, describing the parent's unselfish care for their children, provides one extreme, whereas the other is defined by strategic exchange, in which bequests are solely left in return for services provided by the heir. Even though a mixture of these motives is possible, they are described in isolation below in order to present their specific characteristics in detail.

2.1.2.1 Altruism

The motive of altruistic wealth transfers is based on considerations of Barro (1974) and Becker and Tomes (1979). It is by far the most common bequest motive in literature. Parents are regarded to unselfishly care for the continuance of their dynasty, and are thus anxious about the wealth and wellbeing of future generations. Besides own consumption they hence regard their children's utility level in their own utility considerations. Thus, by varying the amount of wealth transfers, parents try to redistribute their wealth according to their children's own resources. Such compensatory bequests balance the different income opportunities of their children and thus enhance dynastic stability.[21]

Formally, children's utility U_{t+1} is incorporated into the old individual's utility function in addition to own lifetime consumption c^o. This future generation's utility is weighted by the degree of altruism $0 < \beta \leq 1$. It holds that

$$\max U_t = u(c^o) + \beta U_{t+1}.$$

[19] He analyzes the change in consumption as soon as uncertainty about the own lifetime is introduced. Showing that under risk aversion (risk affinity) the rate of consumption decreases (increases) with the mortality rate.

[20] This would imply that the total amount of inheritances would increase with society's survival probability. However, Sexauer (2004) shows that there are two opposing effects released. Sudden death at young age causes the amount of bequests to be higher. On the other hand, the share of individuals surviving until the end of the second period rises. Thereby, the number of individuals increases who dissave entirely, and bequests are less frequent. Hence, both effects neutralize each other. But, within an economy being characterized by unplanned bequests, there might be some optimal survival probability $0 < \theta^* < 1$ for which the amount of bequeathed wealth reaches its maximum.

[21] Reil-Held (2002) shows that children with higher own wealth holding therefore receive less inheritances than a less wealthy sibling.

If assuming that not solely one generation is altruistically linked to its descendants but that rather the entire dynasty pursues altruistic thinking, compensatory bequests would continue from one generation to the other. By regarding the welfare of an entire dynasty, altruism can even obtain an infinite horizon. Due to this reason, Cremer and Pestieau (2006) extend the life cycle theory by the use of recursion, so that old individual's utility reveals

$$\max U_t = \sum_{k=0}^{\infty} \beta^k U_{t+k}. \tag{2.3}$$

For $\beta < 1$, altruism decreases with growing distance between the generations implying that family ties diminish over time.
Budget constraints for parents and children can be written as

$$c^o = e^o - b_t,$$
$$c^y = e^y + (1 + r_{t+1}) I_{t+1},$$

with e^o, e^y describing parent's and children's labor income, respectively. Bequeathed wealth b_t is equivalent to the sum of inheritances I_{t+1} received by the children. The first order condition determining the optimal wealth transfer of the altruistic parent is hence given by

$$\frac{\partial u}{\partial c^o} = \beta \frac{\partial U_y}{\partial c^y}(1 + r).$$

Let $r = 0$, then parents adjust the amount of wealth transferred to their children in order to equal their own marginal utility of consumption and that of their children weighted by β.[22]

Apart from the aforementioned characteristics, altruistic bequests can be further identified by three specific phenomenons. Becker (1974) introduces the *Rotten-Kid-Theorem*, whereby dynastic transfers are considered to exert disciplining effects on the descendants. Hence, even completely egoistic children would have an incentive to increase the total wealth of the family and therefore behave altruistically optimal. This is due to the fact that these children anticipate altruistic behavior of their parents, calculating to reach a higher utility level by means of cooperation than by selfish behavior. Bruce and Waldman (1990) contradict to Becker's considerations by describing the *Samaritan's dilemma*. They identify an incentive problem between parents and their children, supposing that children save

[22] Assuming pure altruism ($\beta = 1$), utility gained by bequeathing corresponds to the utility children receive by consumption.

at lower rates than being dynastically optimal, in order to increase the transfers received from their parents. The last phenomenon, shaped by Barro (1974), is called *Ricardian equivalence*. It implies that altruistic parents will always compensate the intergenerational redistribution of the government. Hence, if expenditures are financed by issuing public debt rather than by taxation, a dynastic parent never consumes her extra savings realized by reduced tax liabilities. Instead, she compensates her children's future debt burden leaving larger bequests.

2.1.2.2 Paternalism

Paternalistic bequests are similar to altruistic thinking, and are therefore often considered as a *reduced form of altruism*.[23] Similarly, testators generate wealth for their descendants without expecting any reward for doing so. However, distinguishing the paternalistic from the altruistic bequest, children's different needs are considered irrelevant.[24] The parent solely incorporates the utility gained by the amount bequeathed, which creates some *joy of giving* that enhances her utility level.[25] This can be determined by

$$\max U_t = u(c^o) + v(b_t),$$

under the budget constraint

$$e_t = c^o + b_t.$$

with $v(\cdot)$ strictly concave, strictly increasing, and twice continuously differentiable. The optimal wealth transfers of paternalistic individuals can thus be derived by the first order condition

$$\frac{\partial u}{\partial c^o} = \frac{\partial v}{\partial b_t}.$$

Maximizing their utility, parents choose the amount of wealth transfers, such that their marginal utility of own lifetime consumption equals the marginal utility generated by warm glow.

Even though paternalism and altruism have much in common, paternalistic implications are less restrictive. Parents refrain from balancing the income opportunities of their children, but instead distribute their wealth equally among them.

[23] See Abel and Warshawsky (1988).

[24] Anything that is unrelated to elephants is irrelephant.

[25] In literature this positive effect on individual's utility is also denoted as *warm glow*.

Moreover, they do not make the effort to compensate their children for government deficits. Generally, paternalistic testators are much more concerned about their own needs. Since bequests can be regarded as an equivalent to consumption goods, paternalism is often also denoted as *bequest-as-consumption* model.

2.1.2.3 Strategic exchange

Ever since, traditional societies transfer wealth among generations as an exchange of payments and services. Parents care for their children until they reach autonomy and additionally transfer wealth and belongings to their descendants at the end of life. In return children usually support their parents, when assistance for reasons of bad health or afflictions of old age is needed. Kotlikoff and Spivak (1981) argue that such pure form of voluntary exchange of services, nowadays, can be found solely in rural regions or developing countries. Therein, family serves as a community to share risks and members safeguard each other.

In modern families, however, parents pointedly use wealth transfers to enforce their needs against their children. They are assumed to gain utility by their descendants' services additionally to own consumption. Children are further regarded to offer assistance solely in return for payments. Thus, parents interlink the amount of their bequests with the intensity of children's attention, such that a strategic motive enters the parental bequest decision.

Bernheim, Shleifer and Summers (1985) consider a non-cooperative game approach to describe this strategic exchange between generations. Therein parents determine a specific amount of wealth to be bequeathed, and additionally lay down how this wealth will be distributed according to the attention given and services performed by each descendant. Children naturally aim to receive the maximum inheritance, however, they have to spend part of their time for their parent in return. Hence, each child balances the costs of leisure or working time losses against the utility gained by inheritance. In the end, a descendant thus offers exactly that extent of attention required to maximize her own utility.[26] Thus, contrary to altruism or paternalism, strategic exchange enables the children to influence the devision of their parent's bequests.[27]

---

[26] Cox (1987) argues the assumption of a cooperative game to be more realistic. In such game, both generations possess bargaining power and are able to be fined when deviating from the optimum. This setting could be modeled by Nash-bargaining or by use of a repeated-game situation with uncertain termination.

[27] See Masson and Pestieau (1997). However, ultimately it is the parent possessing the power to play off her children against each other and to threaten to disinherit those stepping out of line. Thereby, the testator is able to generate the largest benefit for herself.

Under these conditions, a parent maximizes the following utility function, according to lifetime consumption c^o and attention received in old age A:

$$\max U_t = u(c^o) + v(A_{t+1}).$$

The budget constraint for parents and children holds, respectively

$$e^o = c^o + p^A A_{t+1},$$
$$e^y + (1+r)I_{t+1} = c^y,$$

where p^A denotes the price for one unit of attention. Its value equals the cost incurred due to working or leisure time losses. The inheritance, therefore, is a payment for services provided. The optimal amount of wealth transfers can then be defined by use of the first order condition

$$\frac{\partial u}{\partial c^o} p^A = \frac{\partial v}{\partial A_{t+1}}(1+r).$$

Assuming $r = 0$, parents choose an amount of wealth to be inherited, such that the marginal utility of own consumption, multiplied by the price for attention, equals the marginal utility gained by their descendants' attention.

2.1.2.4 Retrospective

The motive of retrospective exhibits some familiar characteristics of other bequest motives – Reil-Held (2002) even speaks of *ad hoc-altruism*. Due to imperfect information and insecurity regarding the future, individuals orientate their own intergenerational transfers towards those having received themselves.

This transfer motive has been analyzed by Cigno (1993) in the case of transfer payments T while alive. However, their characteristics can be similarly applied to wealth transfers occurring at death. In order to reveal the repeated effect, the two-period OLG model has to be extended by a third generation and period. Individuals born in t are assumed to gain utility by consumption c_t^j in each lifetime period $j = 1,2,3$ and hence maximize

$$\max U_t = u(c_t^1, c_t^2, c_t^3).$$

In the second period of life, individuals work and receive labor income e to fund own consumption and that of their parents and children, by means of transfer payments, denoted as T_t^o and T_t^y, respectively. In her first period of life, however, the individual is reliant on the financial support of her parent T_{t-1}^y. In her last period of life, the individual lives on her savings s and hopes for supplementary financial assistance T^o_{t+1} of her on grown-up children. Hence, the budget constraints for these three periods are given by

$$c_t^1 = T_{t-1}^y,$$
$$c_t^2 + T_t^y + T_t^o + s_t = e_t,$$
$$c_t^3 = T_{t+1}^o + (1+r)\, s_t.$$

In her second period of life, the individual has to decide how much transfers to give to parents and children. Anticipating that her descendant will imitate her behavior in the subsequent period, she has to balance present utility losses against expected utility gains. Hence, under these circumstances, transfer payments are indirectly predetermined by family standards which are passed on from one generation to another. The optimal amount of intergenerational transfers can thus be determined by

$$\frac{\partial u/\partial c_t^2}{\partial u/\partial c_t^3} = \frac{T_{t+1}^o}{T_t^y} = \xi,$$

with ξ denoting the interest rate for intra-family credits. It determines how much of given transfers is regained during retirement.[28]

As stated before, these retrospective lifetime transfers are comparable to bequests which are orientated on family standards, predetermining the testator's decision on the amount of wealth transferred. Hence, the testator sets the amount of bequests corresponding to the value having received herself. Therein, the implications of retrospective wealth transfers are quite similar to strategic bequests. Parents also transfer wealth in exchange for services, even though these have been already rendered by the previous generation via bequests. Nonetheless, both motives imply a strategic give-and-take across generations and are thus subsumed under the term of *reciprocal transfers* in the following.

2.1.3 Capitalistic bequests

The motive of capitalistic or entrepreneurial bequests solely emerges among very wealthy individuals, owning wealth too vast to be consumed within a single life-

[28] In this context, Laferrere (2000) argues that parents should decide against having children if investing on the capital market is more profitable. That is the case as soon as the capital market interest rate r is larger than ξ.

time.[29] Evolving a self-augmenting process, such immense wealth holdings often become uncontrollable for their owners. Thus, even though the testator might not be interested in the needs of her family, she has no other possibility than to bequeath most part of her wealth. This idea is even supported by empirical findings, in which significant differences in saving behavior of rich individuals with children, and those without cannot be observed.[30]

Wealthy individuals are assumed to have a desire to leave an immortal vestige of themselves beyond death.[31] Thereby, they do not follow any altruistic beliefs, but instead regard descendants as necessary means to guarantee the survival of their financial or entrepreneurial dynasty.[32] In doing so, they rather institute own foundations or inherit business empires to future generations.

However, being able to explain the bequest motivation of the super-rich, this motive has found scarce interest in the existing literature.

Carroll (1998), and Francis (2008) analyze capitalistic bequests by including the testator's wealth holding directly into the individual's utility function. Thus, they assume that, additionally to private consumption, capitalistic individuals generate utility by the pure existence of wealth w at the end of lifetime. Hence, the maximization problem of a capitalist leads to

$$\max U_t = u(c_o) + v(w_{t+1}).$$

The total derivative produces the first order condition

$$\frac{\partial u}{\partial c_o} = \frac{\partial v}{\partial w}.$$

In equilibrium, capitalistic individuals bequeath exactly that amount of wealth, which equalizes their marginal utility of consumption with the marginal utility of terminal wealth holding.

Contrary, Davies and Shorrocks (2000) argue that capitalistic bequests cannot be described as a result of the pure existence of wealth, but are rather induced by the *desire of immortality*. Thus, the installation of a foundation or the transfer of a business empire could not be reflected by mere monetary wealth at the end of life.

[29] This is due to the fact that individuals do not accumulate growing amounts of wealth, until a critical wealth level is reached. Only above this level, the saving rate continuously increases, and individuals are able to leave capitalistic bequests.

[30] See Hurd (1987), or Kopczuk and Lupton (2007).

[31] This is based on the idea of the 'capitalist spirit'. See Weber (1905).

[32] See Masson and Pestieau (1997).

Similarly, Luo and Young (2009) motivate capitalist's utility to be generated by social status ψ, which is formally incorporated as a luxury good. The capitalistic individual hence maximizes

$$\max U_t = u(c_o) + v(\psi),$$

with $\frac{\partial \psi}{\partial w} > 0$, and $\frac{\partial \psi}{\partial \bar{w}} < 0$. Hence, higher terminal wealth w per se induces higher social status. On the other hand, increasing wealth levels in the direct social environment $\bar{w}$ depreciate the own social status.
In this setting the first order condition can thus be rewritten as

$$\frac{\partial u}{\partial c_o} = \frac{\partial v}{\partial \psi}.$$

The optimal amount of bequest is determined by the marginal utility of consumption that equals the marginal utility of social status.

This dissenting motivation of the very wealthy has received little attention in the optimal tax literature. Therefore, the following sections on normative and positive tax analysis abstract from the capitalistic motive. However, wealth transfers of the very rich constitute the largest share of bequest tax revenues, so that the lack of attention paid to the preferences of the wealthy seems inadequate. The following chapters of this thesis are therefore dedicated to the specific characteristics of capitalistic wealth transfers, evolving the normative, and positive implications in Chapter 3, and 4, respectively.

2.2 Normative analysis of intergenerational wealth transfer taxation

The determination of an optimal tax system in general depends on the existing moral values a society pursues. In this regard, most western countries consider a national duty to achieve an efficient and egalitarian tax system. Therein, it is regarded to be efficient, if individual choices remain undistorted, and disincentives are avoided. Whereas, an egalitarian tax system seeks to obtain an equitable distribution of income, and wealth.

2.2.1 Redistributive vs. allocative effects

The analysis of egalitarian taxation goes hand in hand with the definition of equal sacrifices. Thereby, individuals are considered to be taxed in relation to their ability to pay. Applied to bequest taxation, wealthy individuals are thus to be charged at higher rates to reduce wealth concentration. Hence, the bequest tax seems to be an adequate policy tool to attain a fairer wealth distribution in society. As a consequence, the existence of a wealth transfer tax is often justified by its redistributive impact, and is further invariably associated with enhanced equity.

However, estimating the redistributive effect, it becomes obvious that wealth transfer taxes simultaneously fulfill equity and efficiency considerations in very few instances only. In this regard, following Masson and Pestieau (1997), one has to distinguish between altruistic bequests, and the remaining transfer motives. While the resources are already optimally distributed throughout the generations in a dynastic family, they are not in the remaining cases. Given that individuals, pursuing non-altruistic motives, do not consider the needs of future generations, a tax on bequests can thus be justified for reasons of equity. On the other hand, Scheffler and Wigger (2006) argue that inheritances themselves engender redistribution. This holds true, once wealth is transferred to more than one descendant and when high-income parents transfer wealth to low-income children. Such intrinsic redistribution is endangered as soon as the incentive to bequeath is weakened.

Given these characteristics, the taxation of wealth transfers should not be discussed without considering allocative effects as well. Neglecting behavioral changes of the taxed individuals may even lead to effects opposite to the desired, such that those intended to be supported by redistribution may be adversely affected by this development. How strong these incentive effects turn out to be, is determined by the underlying bequest motive. Thereby, reactions can be twofold. On the one hand, the taxation of estates influences the saving decision of the individual and, on the other hand, may induce even selective tax avoidance.

2.2.1.1 Bequest tax effects on savings

The tax impact on savings is originated in the trade-off between present and future consumption. Whereas this effect is discussed manifold with regard to capital income taxation, an adequate analysis of bequest tax remains barely ignored in literature.

Solely Stiglitz (1978), Bernheim (1999), and to some extent also Gale and Perozek (2000) observe intergenerational wealth transfers with respect to the trade-off between lifetime consumption and savings for bequests. Similar to existing studies on capital income taxation, Stiglitz and Bernheim solely focus on the testator's behavior. Showing that, individuals, planning their bequests, regard transfers less attractive as soon as an estate tax is levied and consequently reduce savings in favor of consumption. Hence, these studies claim that a tax on wealth transfers cause a reduction in wealth formation and thereby a decrease in capital accumulation throughout the entire economy.

However, Gale and Perozek (2000) argue that the estate tax not only affects the behavior of the testators but that of the recipients as well. These are assumed to anticipate the after tax situation by changing both, labor supply and consumption. Ultimately, these changes even impinge on the descendants' saving decision, which possibly may work in opposite direction to parents' behavioral changes. Gale and Perozek therefore recommend incorporating the sum of the testator's and the inheritor's expected tax effects on savings. The results of their analysis depend on the underlying bequest motive.[33]

- Considering **unplanned** bequests the testator's saving decision remains entirely unaffected. However, if descendants anticipate to receive wealth transfers, an estate tax reduces expected receipts and might induce a compensatory increase in own savings. Hence, the aggregated wealth accumulation in society remains invariable or even increases due to estate taxation.

- **Altruistic** parents reduce their savings when being taxed, since bequests become less attractive. Due to the decline in expected transfers, their children will increase their own savings to compensate this loss in inheritance. Hence, the overall effect on wealth accumulation is unclear.

- Regarding **reciprocal** bequests, the estate tax increases the costs parents have to afford for their children's services. In order to keep their children providing the desired level of attention and services, parents have to maintain the net bequest value, and the entire estate tax has to be absorbed by the testators' generation. Hence, if the testators' demand in children's services is inelastic, they have to fund larger inheritances. If reacting elastically instead, testators might substitute their children's attention with consumption of other services. Thereby, savings for bequests are reduced, and consumption is enhanced. In the latter case heirs should anticipate reduced bequests and therefore increase their own provisions by higher savings. Again, the overall effect on capital accumulation in society is undetermined.

- In case of **paternalistic** bequests, parents are assumed to anticipate the *after-tax* amount of bequests according to their demand elasticity of warm glow. Similar to reciprocal bequests, testators thus increase their savings, if their

[33] Gale and Perozek abstract from any redistribution of estate tax revenues, supposing that public transfers always reduce private savings – in the parents' as well as children's generation.

demand is entirely inelastic. On the contrary, they substitute wealth transfers with consumption of other goods, if demand elasticity is high. Due to reduced inheritances, children have to enhance their own savings. Thus, the overall economic effect is again ambiguous. If instead the *pre-tax* value constitutes the basis of decision-making, then parents will remain completely unaffected and saving decisions would be similar to unplanned bequests.

The analysis by Gale and Perozek (2000) thus qualifies the (negative) effects on society's wealth accumulation associated with estate taxation. Empirical investigations, like Joulfaian (2006), show that heirs reduce their savings, when receiving additional wealth transfers. Thus, by implication, heirs should increase their wealth accumulation, if inheritances are expected to decline. However, it is debatable, whether this conclusion can be applied. It can be stated that testators almost always try to reduce their tax burden by enhancing consumption at the expense of savings for future generations. Whereas it is uncertain if the heirs are able to anticipate the reception of a bequest and which amount exactly to inherit. Only with this information available, they are able to adapt to the new situation.

In this regard, Bernheim (1999) argues, it is mainly the testator being able to anticipate changing tax conditions for wealth transfers. Hence, among planned bequests, only children of reciprocally motivated parents can exactly pre-plan the amount of wealth to be inherited. Since both generations bargain with each other they know beforehand the precise bequest value and are able to optimally anticipate their saving behavior. Within all other planned bequest motives a wealth transfer tax, however, provokes a reduction in savings. Resulting in declining wealth accumulation as well as subsiding investments, it hence leads to welfare losses in society.

2.2.1.2 Tax avoidance and migration

Apart from changing consumption and saving decisions, individuals further are able to avoid estate taxation completely. The possibilities to detract capital from tax authorities are manifold, reaching from domestic tax planning activities to migration.

However, tax avoidance activities are costly. Regarding bequest taxation, the expenses depend on total wealth to be inherited as well as on the share that potentially could elude taxation. Therein, Kopczuk and Slemrod (2000) observe relative avoidance costs to decline with increasing wealth holdings. Hence, for wealthy families it may be worth the effort to avoid taxation. It holds that tax avoidance methods are individually profitable as long as the marginal costs are smaller than the marginal estate tax burden.

Domestic avoidance activities are featured by increasing donations, the installation of foundations as well as early gifts to family members.[34] Whereas society, generally, welcomes charitable activities, it challenges gifts during lifetime. The former induces voluntary redistribution without public transfers; the latter by contrast entirely withdraws wealth from reallocation. Usually, however, only altruistic parents consider gifts during lifetime as an alternative to inheritances. This is due to the fact that wealth transfers made early in life, require parents entirely to confide in their children's help and support. By reducing their financial securities, they are reliant upon their descendants' favor in adversity. Further does Nordblom and Ohlsson (2006) show that gifts during lifetime reduce the individuals' utility by lost interest payments and thus diminish future consumption. Given, there is no compensation for this utility loss, behavioral changes induced by estate taxation thus cause inefficiencies, which shall be obviated.[35]

Tax avoidance by migration has to be taken very seriously, since it induces far-reaching economic consequences. Wealthy families leaving for foreign countries, cause domestic capital resources to shrink notably. Thereby, investments decrease and jobs are permanently displaced. Increasing unemployment leads to a declining national wage level and reduces the standard of living. Hence, migration deteriorates the functional income distribution. Due to the arguments of Scheffler and Wigger (2006), migration tendencies are mostly permanent. Once having left the country, individuals very rarely remigrate. Thus, the migration of national tax bases, not only affects state revenues and impairs further redistribution, but entails a series of consequences which notably harm national welfare.

2.2.2 Modeling optimal taxation of bequests

Whether a tax on bequests leads to an excess burden depends on the intensity by which the relative price structure is influenced and to which extent individual behavior is distorted. According to the aforementioned findings, wealth transfers are supposed to react sensitively to taxation. Even though bequest taxes cause inefficiencies, these could be minimized by adequate taxation, taking into account the various characteristics of each bequest motive. In order to evolve an optimal tax system, I assume a simple OLG model with identical agents. Hence, the aggrega-

[34] The opportunity to avoid taxation by lifetime gifts is solely achievable as long as inheritance and gift tax rates deviate.

[35] Most western democracies therefore levy wealth transfer taxes irrespective of whether transfers occurring during lifetime or at death.

tion of the individual utilities weighted by the social time preference rate $0 < \sigma < 1$ leads to the maximization of the entire society's social welfare

$$max \sum_{t=0}^{\infty} \sigma^t U_t. \tag{2.4}$$

The government faces an exogenous budget constraint which is funded by levying a combination of various proportional taxes: a labor income tax τ^l, a capital income tax τ^r, and a tax on bequests τ^b. The corresponding tax rates are then set to maximize the utility of the representative household.

To be able to analyze the tax effect of each of these taxes within the entire tax system, I extend (2.1) and (2.2) by the inclusion of work effort. Thus, individuals receive a labor income e_t that depends on their labor supply l_t. It holds that

$$U_t = u(c_t, c_{t+1}, l_t, b_t), \tag{2.5}$$

with $\partial u(\cdot)/\partial l < 0$ and $\partial u'(\cdot)/\partial l > 0$. The budget constraint of the representative individual can be written as

$$e_t l_t + I_t = c_t + \frac{c_{t+1} + b_t}{1 + r_{t+1}}, \tag{2.6}$$

and the government's budget constraint g is determined by

$$(1+n)\tau_t^l e_t l_t + \tau_t^r (1+r) s_{t-1} + \tau_t^b b_t = g, \tag{2.7}$$

with n denoting population's growth rate.

To define the optimal estate tax rate within the national tax system, the characteristics of each transfer motive are decisive. In doing so, I first of all introduce a traditional OLG model without intergenerational wealth transfers. I then successively extend this basic model to the different bequest motives. Thus, being able to evolve appropriate taxation for each of them.

2.2.2.1 Reference model without bequests

The traditional overlapping generation model according to Diamond (1965) is based on the assumption that individuals dissave wealth completely until their dying day. There is no insecurity about the length of lifetime, since individuals are supposed to live for exactly two periods, consuming in both, but working only in the first. In the absence of intergenerational wealth transfers the government is solely able to fund its budget requirements by the taxation of labor earnings and capital income. In order to establish an optimal combination of these two tax rates, Diamond (1965) states two fundamental results.

- The government is able to redistribute resources across generations by the use of public debt or a pay-as-you-go system. The long-term marginal productivity of capital per capita thus converges to an equilibrium, in which the ratio of population growth equals the time preference rate. This constitutes the so-called *modified golden rule.*
- Although being a dynamic problem, optimal labor and capital income taxes can hence be set according to the rules of the *static* tax theory.

Given these characteristics, the government optimization problem can be written as

$$\max \sum_{t=0}^{\infty} \sigma^t (u(c_t, c_{t+1}, l_t)),$$

subject to the budget constraint, determined in (2.7), with $b_t = 0$. Thus, the optimal tax rates on labor earnings and capital depend on

- the amount of public revenues needed to fund the exogenous budget;
- the compensated elasticities of labor supply and of future consumption;
- the degree of capital accumulation.

Diamond (1965) shows that the elasticities of the tax bases should enter the optimal tax calculus in addition to the required state revenues. If labor is hence inelastically supplied, capital income tax should be set to zero and labor income tax equal to a lump sum tax (and vice versa). However, since most tax bases are not entirely inelastic, generally, a mixture of different tax rates can be observed, which are set according to the particular elasticities.

Moreover, Atkinson and Sandmo (1980) further argue that the use of distorting taxes can be justified, as soon as societies behavior deviates from the equilibrium, determined by the modified golden rule. Imperfect capital accumulation can thus give rise to a tax policy restoring equilibrium in the long run.

2.2.2.2 Unplanned bequests

Due to imperfect asset markets, on the one hand, and lifetime insecurity, on the other, unplanned bequests may occur. However, individuals leaving unplanned bequests do not take into account such accidental transfers in their optimal decision making. Hence, extending the aforementioned reference model to unplanned inheritances, the social planer solely maximizes

$$\max \sum_{t=0}^{\infty} \sigma^t (u(c_t, l_t) + \theta u(c_{t+1})).$$

Given, individual utility is determined by consumption and work effort, Blumkin and Sadka (2003) argue that even a confiscatory tax rate of 100 percent would not create any distortive effects. Thus, following efficiency considerations only, it may be optimal to seize the entire inheritances accidentally transferred to future generations.

Nonetheless, Kopczuk (2002) argues that even if no inefficiencies in the testator's generation are released, there still may be distortions among the heirs. As soon as public revenues gained by the estate tax are redistributed within the descendants' generation, all households receive higher income and thereby aggregate labor supply is reduced. This income effect diminishes the revenues of labor income taxes and shortens further redistribution. Labor income leakages thus compensate the advantages gained by redistribution of the estate tax. Optimizing the gap between these contrary tendencies causes an estate tax rate being high but not compensatory at all. A tax rate of a 100 percent would be optimal if and only if either the optimal income tax amounts to zero or descendants' labor supply is completely inelastic. Hence, the tax rate on unplanned bequests can be determined by:

- the amount of public revenues required;
- the compensated elasticities of descendants' labor supply;
- the optimal tax level on labor income.

According to Cremer and Pestieau (2006) the taxation of unplanned bequests should be preferred over any other income tax. Only if budget requirements exceed potential estate tax revenues, additional capital and labor income taxes shall be levied.

2.2.2.3 Altruism

Altruistic testators already optimize intergenerational welfare by incorporating the utility of future generations into their own utility optimization. Hence, it can be supposed that the intragenerational interest rate, by use of the time preference rate σ, equals the intergenerational interest rate determined by the degree of altruism β. Thus, the government objective function in (2.4) corresponds to that of the altruistic individual in (2.3). Thereby the social welfare function holds

$$\max \sum_{t=0}^{\infty} \beta^t U(c_t, c_{t+1}, l_t). \tag{2.8}$$

Maximizing the welfare function, Chamley (1986) and Judd (1985) argue savings and bequests to remain untaxed in the long run ($\tau^b = \tau^r = 0$). This consideration is simplified by Cremer and Pestieau (2006), who assume the testator's second period consumption to be $c_{t+1} = 0$. By living solely one period, the taxation of wealth transfers thus corresponds to a tax on capital income, which according to Diamond (1965) should not be taxed in the long run.[36] Hence, in the presence of dynastic families with an infinite planning horizon, levying a wealth transfer tax should be determined by one single coefficient:

- the degree of capital accumulation.

In order to reach a new equilibrium, taxation of capital income and hence bequests can be justified within short term transitional periods. Given a steady state always is reached in the long run, permanent capital and wealth transfer taxes should not be levied. Required revenues are thus to be financed by a tax on labor income only.[37]

2.2.2.4 Paternalism

Contrary to altruism, paternalistic testator's utility diverges from the social planner's optimum. However, there is no common consent in literature on how to incorporate joy of giving into the social welfare function. Harsanyi (1995) distinguishes between individual and external preferences. These considerations are based on Dworkin (1977), who determines individual preferences as 'enjoyment of goods and opportunities', whereas external preferences are regarded as 'assignment of goods and opportunities to others'. Harsanyi claims to except the latter that includes the joy of giving motive, from any welfare considerations. On the other hand, utilitarian opinion considers the government to be unauthorized to change or even ignore the preferences of the individuals. Hence, joy of giving has to enter the social planer's welfare maximization calculus entirely.

In order not to limit the analysis of paternalistic bequests to one of these perceptions, Michel and Pestieau (2004) include an additional coefficient $0 \leq \varepsilon \leq 1$

[36] This result remains, even if testators live and consume in two periods, but modeling is much more complicated.

[37] Atkinson and Sandmo (1980) contradict such complete tax exemption. Similarly to Saez (2002) and Fahri and Werning (2006), they argue that due to empirical findings a zero taxation hypothesis solely is viable in a finite planning horizon. With infinity, altruistic wealth transfers would be purely stochastic given that unlimited parental care declines with generation's distance, so that thereby inequality increases. The welfare ambitions of the social planner, in contrast, would remain constant and are thus preferable to dynastic transfers. However, under the above assumption $\sigma = \beta$ this argumentation fails.

into the social welfare function, describing the intensity by which a paternalistic motive is taken into account. This leads to the following social welfare function

$$max \sum_{t=1}^{\infty} \sigma^t [u(c_t, c_{t+1}, l_t) + \varepsilon v(b_t)].$$

For each $\varepsilon > 0$ the optimal amount of wealth transfers is chosen, such that the marginal utility to transfer wealth is equal to zero, $v' = 0$. Hence, the social planer maximizes the bequest value in order to reach the welfare optimum. Different tax rates are thus determined by:

- the amount of public revenues required;
- the degree of capital accumulation;
- the compensated elasticities of labor supply and of future consumption;
- the intensity of ε.

If $v > 0$, old age savings might be exposed to double taxation – by a tax on capital income, on one side, and a tax on bequests, on the other. However, the optimal design of the available taxes is basically defined by ε. For $\varepsilon = 0$ a tax on bequests has to be preferred to all other taxes. The social planer is able to confiscate wealth transfers according to unplanned bequests, without harming social welfare. However, as soon as the social planer includes joy of giving ($\varepsilon > 0$), a tax on bequests must be set in order to minimize individual distortions and thus maximize social welfare. A complete tax exemption or even subsidization is more likely the higher ε.[38]

2.2.2.5 Reciprocal bequests

According to Kaplow (2000), reciprocal wealth transfers resemble the expenses for consumption goods. Hence, bequests should be taxed equally to goods and services. The social planer therefore maximizes

$$max \sum_{t=1}^{\infty} \sigma^t [u(c_t, c_{t+1}, l_t) + v(A_{t+1})].$$

[38]Kaplow (2000) indicates that subsidization might be inefficient, if individuals consider the *pre*-tax amount of bequests rather than the descendants' received net inheritances. In that case parents only regard the own sacrifice for future generations. Subsidization would then reduce the individual sacrifice and therefore diminishes utility.

Given that savings for future bequests are taxed by capital income taxation within lifetime and by a wealth transfer tax at the end of life, such double taxation may induce a higher total tax burden on transferred wealth $\tau^r + \tau^b(1+r)$ than on future consumption. Thus, bequests do not constitute a perfect substitute to consumption goods.

The optimal tax rate on reciprocal bequests hence is determined by:

- the amount of public revenues required;
- the degree of capital accumulation;
- the compensated elasticities of labor supply as well as of future consumption and descendants' attention.

The intensity of estate taxation has to crucially depend on the demand elasticities of future consumption and children's services. Thereby, wealth transfer taxes should be positive (negative) as long as the compensated demand elasticity of descendants' attention is lower (higher) than that of future consumption.

2.2.3 Implications for optimal bequest tax design

The different characteristics of the various bequest motives illustrate the social planer's need for adapting wealth transfer tax rates according to individual incentives to bequeath.

By minimizing the allocative effects subsumed in Table 2.1, government is able to efficiently tax wealth transfers and thereby maximize society's welfare.

- Unplanned bequests might be taxed up to 100 percent. The determination of the estate tax rate depends solely on the potential behavioral response of the heirs. If the recipients' labor supply is elastic bequests shall be taxed heavily but not confiscated completely.
- Pure altruistic bequests shall never be taxed. Given that testators optimally distribute their wealth across generations, social welfare is implicitly maximized at the same time.
- Paternalistic bequests shall remain untaxed or even subsidized as long as $\varepsilon > 0$. Thereby, the value of the estate tax depends on the demand elasticities of warm glow. However, if $\varepsilon = 0$, paternalistic bequests are to be treated like unplanned bequests and thus may be taxed at high rates.

Table 2.1: Effects of wealth transfer taxes according to bequest motives

Incentive effects on...	unplanned	altruistic	paternalistic	reciprocal
testator's saving behavior	none	highly negative	negative/ none*	negative
heir's saving behavior	positive**/ none	positive**/ none	positive**/ none	positive
tax avoidance	none	highly positive	positive/ none*	positive

* for $\varepsilon = 0$

** according to the assumptions of Gale and Perozek (2000)

Source: Following Cremer and Pestieau (2006).

- Reciprocal bequests shall be taxed like future consumption goods. According to the price elasticities of demand, the wealth transfer tax is advised to be positive or even negative.

Hence, in order to design an optimal tax system by means of the aforementioned characteristics, the government ultimately must be able to observe the underlying bequest motive of each inheritance. Although this seems visionary, the government, however, can exploit indications from which to reason the individual bequest motive. In this regard, Scheffler and Wigger (2006) argue that bequests made to close relatives, like own spouses or children, are much more indicative of a dynastic motive than those made to distant family members or even strangers. Similarly, Richter (1987) motivates that, in addition to value, bequests should be taxed according to the degree of consanguinity between inheritor and heir. Accordingly, tax rates are lower the closer the family ties.

As a result, optimal taxation of bequests shall allow for individual tax exemptions rather than for special treatment of specific assets. Only then will it be possible to align towards the different needs of each bequest motive and hence to optimize tax policy.

2.3 Political-economic analysis of intergenerational wealth transfer taxation

All findings of Section 2.2 are based on normative considerations, determining the optimal wealth transfer taxation that maximizes social welfare. However, these results change as soon as a legislative process with self-interested political agents is incorporated.

Relating to this, Brennan and Buchanan (1977) show that such *leviathan state* strives to maximize own revenues rather than society's welfare. To receive legitimization for its policies, its main objective therefore is to attract majoritarian votes, which succeeds best, if individuals are unable to judge the amount of taxes they pay (fiscal illusion). Moreover, state revenues are utilized to promote those public projects, generating the largest political support.

Similarly, Hettich and Winer (1984) argue, selfish political agents therefore choose precisely that tax structure that minimizes their political costs. Thus, given an exogenous budget constraint, the potential loss of votes has to be optimized.

Both concepts reveal that collective choice may distort the normative optimal tax implications. Regarding wealth transfer taxes, however, there is little literature on political-economic considerations. Solely Aura (2004) observes the positive implications of an estate tax within a democracy. Using an OLG model with homogeneous individuals, who are altruistically linked to their descendants, he shows that against normative implications taxation of wealth transfers might be politically optimal. This section concentrates on altruistic wealth transfers only, as no literature exists covering up to which extent other bequest motives may lead to distortions from the normative optimal solution.

2.3.1 Politically optimal taxation of bequests

In order to illustrate the preferences and voting behavior of each generation, the OLG model of the previous normative analysis is extended to two dynasties A and B. These dynasties live simultaneously, but lagged by one period (Figure 2.1).

By this construction, always one dynasty's event of death, and therewith wealth transfer, lies in very distant future. Their short term planning horizon is not determined by savings for their descendants, but rather by own future consumption.

The government is assumed to generate its revenues by taxes on labor earnings, capital income, and bequests. According to Aura (2004), the government's budget has to be balanced at all times, however, the determination of tax policy is endogenized by repeated referenda. Each period the individuals therefore have to vote

Figure 2.1: Time path of the individual decision process

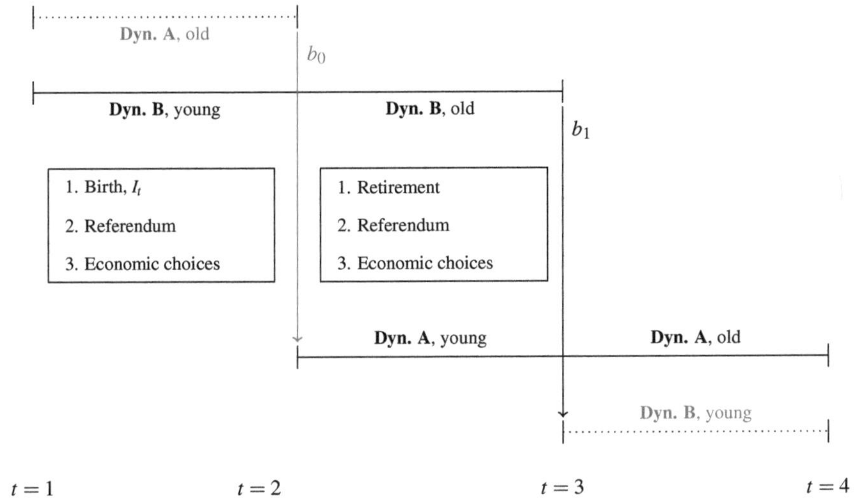

on distinct tax rates, defining the optimal policy according to political majorities. To simplify matters, individual labor supply is considered to react inelastically and hence labor income to be taxed lump sum. Voters are assumed to have to decide on the tax rate on wealth transfer, and the required capital income tax is successively chosen to balance the budget. In doing so, individuals are supposed to have perfect information on the decision process and are able to predict future tax rates as a function of today's choices.

At the beginning of life, the individual receives an inheritance I_t. Subsequently, she votes on the tax policy and chooses optimal consumption and saving c_t, s_t in accordance with the voting result. With transition into the second period the individual retires and is again asked to vote on the tax rates. Given the tax environment, she then determines optimal consumption c_{t+1} and savings for bequests b_t, which are entirely motivated by altruistic care for the own dynasty.

According to Winer and Hettich (2002) the results of collective choice can be analyzed by use of the median-voter model as well as by probabilistic voting.

The **median-voter** theorem traces back to Black (1958), who argues the politically optimal tax policy to be the result of majoritarian decisions in direct voting processes. Therein he abstracts from any strategic behavior and insecurity regarding the voting results, such that any individual opts for that policy which maximizes her welfare. In order to receive unequivocal results this theorem can only be applied as long as individuals vote on solely one single parameter, for which they exhibit single-peaked preferences.

To derive the median-voter equilibrium for the taxation of wealth transfers in the present setting, voting society has to be divided in young and old voters. The young generation is directly affected by an estate tax already at birth. However, even though their inheritances are reduced by taxation, they do not have the possibility to influence the tax rate, since wealth was transferred before the new referendum took place. After the inheritance receipt, young and old individuals together vote on the estate tax rate and thereby at the same time implicitly determine present capital income taxation.

Within this model the voting process leads to the result that all young individuals will vote for the installation of a wealth transfer tax, whereas all old individuals, prefer a tax on capital income. The young will *not yet* be affected by a tax on bequests in the near future, whereas a tax on capital earnings affects them directly today. Therefore they oppose the latter and favor the taxation of bequests, passing the tax burden to the other (old) dynasty. Within this calculus, young individuals anticipate to be asked to vote again in the next period and thereby consider the opportunity to be able to revise their decisions made today. The old, on the contrary, vote for the lowest possible bequest tax rate, in knowledge of their death at the end of this period. In which case a tax on wealth transfers directly reduces their altruistic utility gained by bequeathing to their descendants. A tax on capital earnings, however, does not affect them anymore, since savings have already been taxed in the previous period. They thereby attempt to pass the tax burden to other (young) dynasty.[39]

However, disregarding all other individuals, ultimately, the preferences of the median-voter determines current tax policy. Hence, assuming a homogeneous society with positive population growth, the median-voter will always be a young individual. Contrary to normative theory, the estate tax will be set at positive rates in every period. The median passes the costs of public spending to the other, the old, dynasty.

By use of a **probabilistic-voting** model, it can be shown that wealth transfers also are to be taxed in the political equilibrium, however the dominant effect constituted by the median-voter approach vanishes. Following Persson and Tabellini (2000), two parties are supposed to compete for votes, with neither the young nor the old voting cohort preferring any of the two parties per se. Further all voters of both generations are similarly mobile in their voting behavior. Based on these

[39]These observations follow the implications of intergenerational tax incidence. See Wigger (2004).

assumptions, the two parties maximize the social welfare function, weighting the utilities of each generation by the share of young and old in society, which is denoted by n_y, n_o, respectively. Hence, it holds

$$max\, W = n_o U_A + n_y U_B. \tag{2.9}$$

By assumption of positive population growth ($n_y > n_o$), tax policy gives greater emphasis to young voters' preferences. However, the old generation's preferences influence tax policy as well. Thus, under probabilistic-voting, the result is not as incisive as in the median-voter approach, but its impact remains.

In result, both scenarios justify the positive taxation of wealth transfers and cause the political optimal tax rate to deviate from the normative implications. This is due to imperfect policy commitment, which enables the individuals to re-optimize political decisions every period. It can be shown that the shorter these voting periods, the larger the deviation from the normative optimum. If the assumption of sequential voting is replaced by once-for-all voting, the results change completely. Given that voters have to decide upon the tax rate once up to infinity, they anticipate that readjustment of political decisions is impossible. In which case, once-for-all voting causes the normative result to be politically optimal as well. Hence, under the absence of regular voting periods, altruistic bequests are exempted from taxation even in the political equilibrium.

2.3.2 Extensions

The political-economic implications of the previous analysis essentially depend on positive population growth as well as on the homogeneity of individuals. Hence, it is interesting to observe, how this political equilibrium can be modified, if allowing for changes in society's age composition as well as for the existence of heterogeneous agents.

Society's aging is a serious challenge for most industrialized countries. Applied to intergenerational wealth transfers, higher life expectancy combined with lower birth rates, leads to changing preferences of each individual as well as of the entire society. Therein, individuals reveal an intensified consumption at older age, such that the testators' generation evolves into a cohort of high spending power and increased dissaving. Due to higher life expectancy, bequests take place later in life and consequently are inherited by those individuals already having reached retirement age themselves. Regarding these aspects, Reil-Held (2002) discusses intergenerational wealth transfers as an alternative to the traditional pay-as-you-go old age security. Contrarily, Szydlik (2004) on the other hand argues that with increasing age, testators bequeath their wealth directly to their grandchildren. Given their own children have already reached secured retirement, the incentive to care for their wellbeing has become unappealing. However, demographic change also leads to changing structures in society and thereby to new political majorities. As wealth transfer taxes affect solely old individuals, which, under the assumption of lower birth rates, gain increasing political weight, the political equilibrium is expected to change.

Although there is no specific literature on aging with regard to bequest taxation, demographic impacts analyzed for the taxation of capital can be transferred. Therefore, Razin, Sadka and Swagel (2002) show that the median-voter's transition from young to old age is likely to increase labor income taxes as well as the demand for public social services. In a later approach, Razin and Sadka (2007) modify this consideration, by extending the analysis to capital income taxes, implying that aging does not necessarily causes tax revenues to increase and the welfare state to expand. Similarly, Mateos-Planas (2010) supposes a negative correlation of increasing society's average age and the tax rate on capital income. However, he detects an additional countervailing equilibrium effect, leading to the acceptance of capital income taxes even among the old.[40]

These results can be applied to intergenerational wealth transfers, which – like capital taxation – solely affect the old generation. However, avoidance possibilities differ. Whereas capital income is predetermined in the previous period, the proportion of savings to be bequeathed is not. Thus, these savings might be entirely withdrawn, when being taxed too heavily. In a homogeneous society population's aging therefore is supposed to induce lower bequest tax rates in equilibrium.

Extending the model to a society being heterogeneous according to wealth, differences in tax preferences as well as in opportunities to exercise **political influence** of specific individuals or groups become relevant. Under these circumstances, supporters and opponents of wealth transfer taxes can no longer be distinguished solely by age, but additionally by wealth level. Whereas rich individuals reject an estate tax, individuals with little or even no wealth holdings favor its taxation for sake of redistribution. Such division into opponents and supporters across the age levels offers the opportunity for pressure groups to gain political influence. Even though no specific literature addresses this problem with regard to

[40]This effect is based on factor prices of labor and capital. Aging of society leads to a capital surplus and a workforce deficit. Thereby the interest rate decreases whereas the wage rate increases. Compensatory taxes on capital income are thus preferred among the old and young. Using an empirical evidence of the historical evolution of tax rates in the US since 1965, Mateos-Planas shows that this equilibrium effect even predominates. The rejuvenation of the American society between 1965 and 1990 led to a decline of capital income taxation, whereas the projected aging between 1990 and 2025 is expected to increase capital income taxation.

wealth transfer taxation, the ideas of Becker (1983) are suitable to explain expected political adjustments. It is assumed that both dynasties A, B consist of wealthy individuals ($b > 0$) and those without means ($b = 0$). Therein, a tax on bequests affects the wealthy individuals, whereas the impecunious gain by redistribution of tax revenues. Differentiating further between young and old voters, the young dynasty favors the taxation of estates, independently of its wealth level. Among the old dynasty, the wealthy prefer a capital income tax, whereas the impecunious are indifferent.

	$b > 0$	$b = 0$
old	$\tau^r \succ \tau^b$	indifferent
young	$\tau^b \succ \tau^r$	$\tau^b \succ \tau^r$

A pure observation of majorities implies the old, wealthy voters to be outright losers and the young dynasty, regardless of being rich or poor, to be outright winners of the political process. It is, however, conceivable that losers will not simply accept this tax policy, but rather try to reduce their losses by targeted lobbying. Thereby, it can be shown that political power and influence of pressure groups may be quite ambiguous. Following Becker (1985), the intensity of public redistribution is not determined by maximization of the social welfare function, but instead shaped by altruism, egoism, envy or moral of the strongest pressure group. Coughlin, Mueller and Murrell (1990) model the political influence of a pressure group within a two-party approach under probabilistic voting. Therein, the individual utility of each society member is not incorporated equally like in (2.9), but weighted by different coefficients that determine the political decision making. Transferring these results to the politically optimal taxation of wealth transfers, winners and losers are supposed to form pressure groups according to their specific tax preferences. In the first period, government faces two pressure groups $i = A_o, B_y$ – the former represents the interest of the old, wealthy individuals of dynasty A, the latter aggregates the interests of all young agents of dynasty B. The influence of each group is assumed to increase with the number of members η_i, the homogeneity of interests within each group χ_i as well as with the intensity of their potential political pressure z_i.[41]

[41] Interest group homogeneity is defined by $\chi_i = 1/(l_i - r_i)$, with the denominator defining the bias of individual preferences – left, l_i, and right, r_i – within the group. Political pressure z_i is supposed to increase with financial possibilities, public visibility, and the credibility of tax avoidance opportunities.

Thus, the political parties maximize

$$max\, W = \chi_{A_o} n_{A_o} z_{A_o} U_{A_o} + \chi_{B_y} n_{B_y} z_{B_y} U_{B_y}.$$

It can be supposed that the young dynasty gains political influence due to its size. However, the old, wealthy individuals are able to use their political pressure to influence the government decisions in their own favor. Political influence of old, economically powerful individuals, moreover, is expected to rise with society's aging and increasing wealth inequality, contributing the bargaining power of the very rich.

2.4 Concluding remarks

The review of the literature indicates that an assessment of a universal optimal wealth transfer tax is quite complex. As a result, neither unconditional supporters nor vehement opponents are supposed to be on the right track. The former often neglect behavioral responses of heirs. Provoking capital flight, overall tax revenues are reduced. Hence, the excessive taxation of wealth transfers might even impair the situation for those meant to benefit from redistribution. Vehement opponents, however, ignore the additional potential for redistribution, gained by taxation of unplanned bequests. Furthermore, they disregard the political implications pleading for a wealth transfer tax. In conclusion an optimal bequest tax rate should be focused on the underlying motive each testator pursues when transferring wealth. Such differentiated taxation might enable to jointly fulfill a series of normative as well as positive criteria.

Nevertheless, bequest motives are hard to identify and furthermore usually do not exist in pure form. However, for practical application of the aforementioned findings, a classification system is needed to be able to categorize different bequests. Thus, one can argue that wealth transfers to own spouses or direct descendants might be much more dynastically motivated than those to distant relatives. Hence, the amount of personal tax reliefs should be expanded. An additional complete tax exemption of spouses and children would be advisable. Thereby, the continuation of family property and enterprises would be guaranteed, such that a special tax treatment for specific assets would become obsolete.

In order to be politically viable, the taxation of large bequests should be continued, since the beneficiaries of redistributive payments outnumber those affected by taxation. However, it should be noted that political influence of the wealthy counteracts their numerical inferiority. In the future, population's aging and increasing international tax competition will further promote the bargaining power of the wealthy.[42] Political agents, therefore, need to adjust their optimal tax policy to these new conditions.

On grounds of these findings, there is still a great need identified for further research on wealth transfer taxation. Therein, special attention must be paid to capitalistic bequests. Even though this motive has been revealed to be able to explain the saving behavior of the very wealthy, neither normative nor positive implications for the optimal bequest taxation of the very rich have been explored. Yet in many industrialized countries wealth transfer taxes are imposed solely on the very rich, such that precisely their preferences and behavioral responses have to be taken into account when evaluating tax policy. In the course of the following chapters, I therefore deal with the optimal taxation of capitalistic bequests, answering

- up to which extent wealth transfers of the very rich should be taxed in *economic equilibrium*, anticipating a society characterized by heterogeneity in age and wealth,
- which tax rates on bequests of the very wealthy are *politically viable* under majority rule in such a heterogeneous society, as well as
- how current bequest tax policy can be assessed, by application of the aforementioned findings.

[42]The European right of unrestricted mobility further boosts international tax competition. Even though tax-induced migration of very wealthy families seems to be omnipresent in the media, there is little empirical evidence, indicating the extent of testators' reactions when being taxed. For the US there are some basic approaches quantifying the extent of estate tax avoidance, like e.g. in Bakija and Slemrod (2004). Nevertheless, due to specific assumption, the results of these studies differ widely.

3 Normative aspects of taxing capitalistic bequests

"Let me tell you about the very rich. They are different from you and me. They possess and enjoy early, and it does something to them, [...] in a way that, unless you were born rich, it is very difficult to understand."

F. Scott Fitzgerald (in "The rich boy")

Bequest motives serve as an explanation why individuals do not decumulate assets completely during retirement, and some even continue saving while old. Nevertheless, common family-oriented bequest models still fail to account for the saving behavior of the very wealthy, among which a significant difference between those with children and those without cannot be observed.[43]

Empirical work of Arrondel and Laferrère (2001), De Nardi (2004), and Dynan, Skinner and Zeldes (2004) has shown that the upper tail of the wealth distribution reveals different patterns of saving. Even though wealth accumulation of the very rich is highly relevant for the economy, it still has received little attention in theoretical academic literature. Solely Zou (1994), Carroll (1998), and Francis (2008) incorporate a wealth creating ambition, by including terminal wealth into the very wealthy's utility function. On the contrary, Davies and Shorrocks (2000) and Luo and Young (2009) argue that very rich individuals do not derive utility from terminal wealth but from the "desire of immortality". Despite their differences, both approaches indicate why many fortunes end up in charitable foundations which, in contrast to own descendants, often better accomplish benefactor's will.

Assuming that, with increasing wealth, individuals rather dedicate utility to the immortality of own lifework and property than to family concerns, this chapter analyzes the preferences of rich individuals – referred to as 'capitalists' – their motives to save and to bequeath and the impact of a wealth transfer tax on their behavior. Therefore, Section 3.1 reveals why the standard life cycle model as well as wealth transfer models, focusing on family concerns, cannot explain the consumption and savings decision of the wealthy. Section 3.2 develops a 'capitalist

[43] See Hurd (1987) and Kopczuk and Lupton (2007). Hurd interprets his findings with the absence of a bequest motive, whereas Kopczuk and Lupton still find evidence of an operative bequest motive.

spirit' model in which the wealthy gain utility directly by holding assets and by passing them on to following generations. Focus lies on behavioral changes as well as on social welfare implications released by estate taxation. Section 3.3 extends the model to the existence of foundations. Finally, Section 3.4 concludes.

3.1 Life-cycle savings and family bequests – an explanation for transfers of the rich?

Following the 'proportionality hypothesis' of Friedman (1957), consumption and savings ratios are independent from permanent income. Implying there is no saturation in consumption, one may suggest wealthy individuals behave identical to any other society member.

Empirical findings apparently contradict this hypothesis, exhibiting that especially rich individuals barely reduce funds when old and prevailing unanimous belief about the difference in saving ratios between recipients of high and relatively low permanent income.[44] One could argue this is due to the fact that the amount of wealth and interests gained is too vast to be consumed within a single lifetime. According to Modigliani (1986) one could, on the other hand, assert saving being a luxury good, causing higher saving rates among the rich. In order to further analyze the bequest motives of the wealthy, their saving behavior is compared to the pure life cycle theory as well as to family-oriented savings, showing that the common bequest motives fail to explain the behavior of the upper tail of the wealth distribution.

Intragenerational accumulation of savings basically can be described by the standard life cycle model developed by Modigliani and Brumberg (1954). It defines consumption and saving decisions of forward looking individuals, whose preferences are defined over present and future consumption, incorporating a period of retirement at life's end. The accumulation of wealth is thereby solely driven by the individuals' desire to optimize rewards of consumption. The age-profile of wealth holding is expected to have a hump-shape with its peak occurring near the date of retirement and a complete decumulation of wealth until death. Empirical findings, however, reveal that a large fraction of society dies with positive personal wealth (Figure 3.1). Extensions to the basic life cycle model therefore incorporate, for example, capital market imperfections or uncertainty in earnings and in length of lifetime, which are given as explanation for the existence of unplanned

[44] Friedman's assumption has caused a long controversial in the literature, generating opponents as well as supporters. See Kotlikoff and Summers (1981).

Figure 3.1: Individual wealth over lifetime: life-cycle theory vs. empirical findings

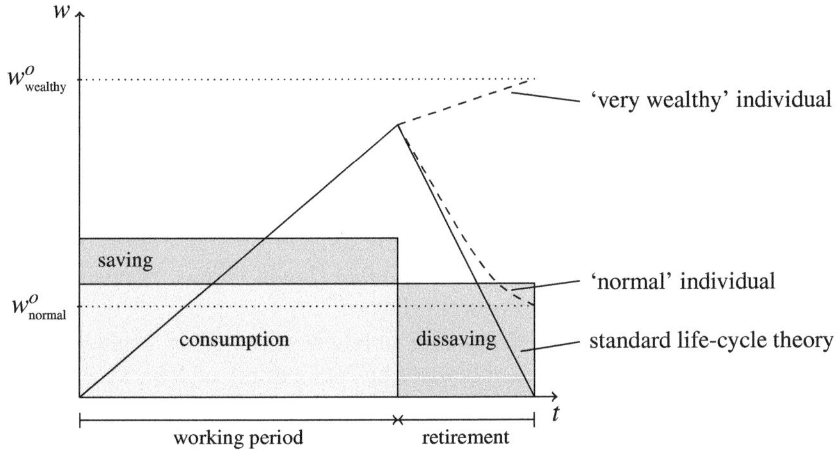

bequests. Nevertheless, theories of lifetime accumulation and accidental bequests, caused by the lack of planning reliability, are quite inadequate for those individuals having made a sizable fortune during lifetime. Contradicting the argumentation of unplanned bequests, De Nardi (2004) demonstrates that rich individuals often continue working even though having accumulated enough wealth to live in extreme luxury until the end of life.

Positive wealth holdings at the time of death can further be originated by direct family-oriented bequest motives – already described in Chapter 2.1 – generating utility by the transference of wealth to future generations. Savings are regarded not only for *intra*generational purposes by smoothing consumption over time, but also for *inter*generational issues and might thus explain even the saving behavior of the very rich.

However, first notably since Hurd (1987) and Laitner and Juster (1996) revealed that sizable bequests generally are independent of the existence and number of children, it has become evident that pure family concerns cannot be responsible for the absence of wealth decumulation in retirement. Furthermore, Carroll (1998) and De Nardi (2004) show that neither unselfish parental care nor strategic motives appear to be very strong for those having made a remarkable fortune, given that the rich mostly leave the bulk of their wealth to charity rather than to their children. Thus altruistic preferences, characterized by compensatory bequest equalizing welfare among the descendants, as well as a strategic motive, in which wealth is transferred as payment for services delivered by the donee, cannot account for the very wealthy's preferences.

Among the common bequest motives, paternalism, pursuing the idea of warm glow (or joy of giving), provides the closest fit to explain wealth transfers of the wealthy. Since giving itself produces a benefit to the donor without incorporating the effects on the donee, utility is derived by the amount of terminal wealth transferred. Similarly, for the very rich it is wealth itself or its associated attributes, which induce a motivation to save at even increasing rates until death. Though, deviating from 'joy of giving', sizable wealth already generates utility in all periods of life and even beyond death – a fact that should be incorporated into the modeling of the very wealthy's bequest behavior.

The importance of such wealth creating ambition – denoted as 'capitalist spirit' – has long been recognized by economists like Adam Smith or John M. Keynes as the underlying driving force for economic growth. They were aware that wealth serves to advertise status as well as to achieve higher social positions and power during life, inducing individuals to undertake growth-enhancing economic activities. The perception that this motivation continues beyond death and can thus be reflected even in bequest behavior was first adumbrated by Atkinson (1980). He argued that the transfer motives of those individuals having gained substantial wealth by entrepreneurial activity differ from classical bequest motivations. In this regard Hurd (1987), Masson and Pestieau (1997), and Arrondel and Laferrère (2001) also refer to a 'capitalist spirit' suggesting a prime motivation of the rich to see their name continued in the public arena even beyond death.

3.2 The Model

Analyzing the effects of a wealth transfer tax on bequests of the very wealthy and demonstrating its relevance for society, a simple overlapping generation model is introduced with just the essential features needed to describe the characteristics of the 'capitalist spirit'.

Suppose there are two dynasties $i = L, H$ each consisting of two generations which both live for two periods. During the first period of life, the individuals work, consume, and save. In the second period the individuals retire and live off their savings, which they spend for own consumption and bequests.

Each parent, born in t, has a single child, born in $t+1$, to whom she leaves all her remaining wealth. Consumption and savings are denoted with c^y, c^o, w^y, w^o for young and old respectively. Each individual is endowed with one unit of time in

Figure 3.2: Time path of the model

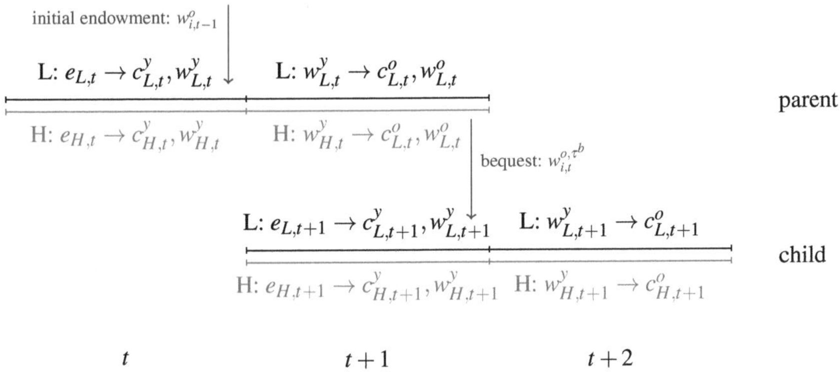

her first period of life, which she can spend for working. The chosen labor supply l_i determines foregone leisure denoted by $1-l_i$. Further, the dynasties differ in innate earning abilities, with $p_L < p_H$. Both, labor supply (effort) and innate ability are unobservable. Information on the individual's gross income only exists as product of effort and ability $e_i = p_i l_i$, where $e_L < e_H$ holds. The government imposes a non-linear income tax, such that the individuals receive a net income x_L, x_H, and additionally a proportional tax on bequests τ^b.

Individuals, in general, are assumed to be life cycle savers. However, above a critical wealth threshold a, individuals of the parent generation are supposed to follow a 'capitalist spirit' motive. In that case, they gain additional utility by wealth holding during periods alive $w^y_{i,t}, w^o_{i,t}$ as well as by the survival of their wealth within the following generation. This wealth transfer may be taxed by the government and is denoted by $w^{o,\tau^b}_{i,t}$. Individuals hence maximize:

$$U_i(c,w,l) = u(c^y_{i,t}) + \gamma v(w^y_{i,t}) + h(1-l_i) + \frac{u(c^o_{i,t}) + \gamma v(w^o_{i,t})}{1+\sigma} + \gamma \frac{v(w^{o,\tau^b}_{i,t})}{(1+\sigma)^2}, \quad (3.1)$$

with $u(\cdot)$, $v(\cdot)$, and $h(\cdot)$ strictly concave, strictly increasing, and twice continuously differentiable. The parameter σ describes the time-preference rate and $\gamma \geq 0$ denotes the degree of the 'capitalist spirit' determining the emphasis given to the wealth term.[45] In the following, I first analyze the individual optimum lifetime de-

[45] With $\gamma = 0$ the model reduces to a standard precautionary saving's model, which occurs with wealth holding below a.

cision process in the parent's generation, characterizing the distortive effects that emerge with the imposition of an estate tax. In a next step, social welfare considerations of a benevolent government are incorporated, taking into account both generations and dynasties.

3.2.1 Individual optimum bequest decision

Suppose, agents of dynasty $i = L, H$ earn a positive, exogenous net income $x_{i,t}$ when young. Additionally, they receive a (differing) wealth transfer $w^o_{i,t-1}$ from the previous generation. Assuming for simplicity that high-able individuals have high-able ancestors, these are endowed with more initial wealth and thereby will leave larger bequests to the following generation.[46] Once retired the individuals live off their savings. Thus, I maximize (3.1) under the following budget constraints

$$w^y_{i,t} = x^y_{i,t} + w^o_{i,t-1} - c^y_{i,t}, \tag{3.2}$$

$$w^o_{i,t} = w^y_{i,t} - c^o_{i,t}. \tag{3.3}$$

In equilibrium, parents consume and save in both periods so that

$$c^y_{i,t} : u'(c^y_{i,t}) = \gamma v'(w^y_{i,t}) + \frac{1}{1+\sigma} u'(c^o_{i,t}), \tag{3.4}$$

$$c^o_{i,t} : u'(c^o_{i,t}) = \gamma v'(w^o_{i,t}) + \gamma \frac{1}{1+\sigma} v'(w^{o,\tau^b}_{i,t}). \tag{3.5}$$

Contrasting to pure life cycle considerations, where savings solely serve to finance future consumption, wealth creates additional utility by its existence per se. Thus, the marginal utility of first period consumption has to equal the marginal utility of future consumption weighted with the time preference rate plus the marginal utility gained by wealth holding weighted with the rate of 'capitalist spirit'. When old, the marginal utility to consume equals the sum of marginal utilities derived by present wealth holding and by its survival within the future dynasty, both weighted with γ. Thus, the intensity to consume when young and old is determined by the factor of 'capitalist spirit'. The higher it is, the higher are wealth preferences and the lower is consumption.

In order to give further evidence regarding the individual lifetime utility, an assumption about the concrete functional form of utility is needed. In the following,

[46] The assumption of the positive correlation of initial wealth and abilities appears plausible, given that empirical findings show that individuals with higher income also own more wealth and a substantial part of this wealth is regarded to inheritances. See Gale and Scholz (1994) and Modigliani (1988).

I use a standard CRRA form for the consumption and the leisure term and a modified Stone-Geary form for the wealth term. Entering both additively into the utility function leads to

$$U_i = \frac{(c^y_{i,t})^{1-\mu}}{1-\mu} + \gamma \frac{(w^y_{i,t}+a)^{1-\phi}}{1-\phi} + \frac{(1-l_i)^{1-\mu}}{1-\mu} + \frac{\frac{(c^o_{i,t})^{1-\mu}}{1-\mu} + \gamma \frac{(w^o_{i,t}+a)^{1-\phi}}{1-\phi}}{1+\sigma} + \gamma \frac{\frac{(w^{o,\tau b}_{i,t}+a)^{1-\phi}}{1-\phi}}{(1+\sigma)^2}, \tag{3.6}$$

where μ denotes relative risk aversion for consumption and leisure, and ϕ controls the curvature of the wealth term. Further $a > 0$ is defined as a modified Stone-Geary parameter, assuring that for initial consumption the marginal utility to consume is strictly greater than the marginal utility to accumulate wealth, and thereby generating heterogeneity in the demand for wealth.[47]

In the following, I assume for simplicity that $\mu = \phi = 1$. By use of L'Hôpital's rule the utility terms in (3.6) become logarithmic.[48]
Solving the maximization problem in (3.6) with respect to the budget constraints (3.2) and (3.3), optimal consumption reveals, when old and young respectively

$$c^{o*}_{i,t} = \frac{(w^y_{i,t}+a)(1+\sigma)}{1+\sigma+\gamma(2+\sigma)}, \tag{3.7}$$

$$c^{y*}_{i,t} = \frac{(w^o_{i,t-1}+x+a)(1+\sigma)^2}{2+3\sigma+\sigma^2+\gamma(3+3\sigma+\sigma^2)}. \tag{3.8}$$

As the marginal utility of wealth is lower for initial consumption levels, individuals with a low permanent income would even choose to die in debt.[49] Therefore a *no-borrowing* constraint has to be added, to guarantee that wealth is nonnegative in both periods

$$c^y_{i,t} + c^o_{i,t} \leq x^y_{i,t} + w^o_{i,t-1}, \tag{3.9}$$

leading to the following proposition.

[47] This modified parameter is similar to the original Stone-Geary parameter which, describing a subsistence minimum in consumption, is negative in the formulations of Stone (1954) and Geary (1949-50). The modified form in this model, however, is positive, determining the relative scale over which the 'capitalist spirit' outweighs the individual's impatience and desire for immediate consumption.

[48] $\lim_{\mu \to 1} \frac{(c^y_{i,t})^{1-\mu}}{1-\mu} = (1-\mu)\frac{(c^y_{i,t})^{1-\mu-1}}{-\mu} = \ln(c^y_{i,t})$; equivalently, this holds for all other utility terms.

[49] Thereby increasing the marginal utility of wealth and lower that of consumption.

Proposition 1. *The solution to the individual maximization problem is given by*

$$c_{i,t} = min[(c_{i,t}^{y,*} + c_{i,t}^{o,*}), (w_{i,t} + x_{i,t})].$$

Lifetime consumptions $c_{i,t}$ is hence determined by the minimum of the sum of optimal consumption in both periods and the sum of labor income and inheritances.

Proof. Consider a low-able individual with $w_{i,t-1}^{o} + x_{i,t} < a$. Due to the assumption that the wealth term is described by a modified Stone-Geary form, for low consumption levels it holds $u'(c) > v'(w+a)$. Hence, without a no-borrowing constraint all parents with permanent income smaller than a would borrow to increase consumption. ■

The no-borrowing constraint is binding for all agents with wealth holdings below the threshold level a. These individuals are life cycle savers, decumulating all assets until death. Contrasting, agents above the threshold level will save and leave behind wealth at ever increasing rates as permanent income rises.

3.2.1.1 Special case – optimal bequest decision

The results obtained so far are illustrated in the following numerical example.

Example 3.1. Let for the above concrete utility function $\mu = \phi = 1$, such that $u = \ln(c_{i,t})$ and $v = \ln(w_{i,t} + a)$, and assume $\sigma = 0.1$. Let further, initial wealth and net income for dynasty $H : w_{t-1}^{o} = 10, x_t = 10$ and $L : w_{t-1}^{o} = 0, x_t = 3$.[50]

When varying the threshold levels a and the strength of 'capitalist spirit' γ there are three observations to be made (Table 3.1).

- High-able individuals with permanent income above the threshold level a, one the one hand, reduce consumption with increasing γ.

- A higher threshold level a, on the other hand, causes high-able individuals to diminish savings and to increment consumption.

[50] To solve the model, I begin with determining the last period consumption. Given that the individual might choose to die with positive wealth holding, last period consumption is not determined by remaining assets of the previous period, as in the typical life-cycle problem. Instead, optimal consumption in the last period is denoted by $c_{i,t}^{o,*} = w_{i,t-1}^{o} + x_{i,t} - c_{i,t}^{y,*} - w_{i,t}^{o,*}$. If the individual's permanent income, $w_{i,t-1}^{o} + x_{i,t}$, is small, the consumer will want to die in dept, which is restricted by (3.9). Thus, lifetime consumption $c_{i,t}$ is smaller or equal to the given individual budget.

Table 3.1: Exemplary optimal bequest decision under non-taxation

		γ	$c_{i,t}^{y,*}$	$w_{i,t}^{y,*}$	$c_{i,t}^{o,*}$	$w_{i,t}^{o,*}$
$i = H$	$a = 5$	1.1	5.0831	14.9169	6.4247	8.4922
		1.5	4.1580	15.8420	5.3944	10.4476
	$a = 7$	1.1	5.4898	14.5102	6.9388	7.5714
		1.5	4.4907	15.5093	5.8259	9.6834
$i = L$		0	1.5714	1.4286	1.4286	0

- In contrast, low-able individuals would rather die in dept to increase consumption levels. In this case, the no-borrowing constraint is binding. Low-able individuals become life cycle savers, leaving no bequests to their descendants. Given that $\gamma = 0$ and irrespective of the threshold level a, low-able individuals will only smooth consumption over time.

Suppose now, the social planner intervenes in the decision process, imposing a tax on wealth transfers $\tau^b > 0$. Thus, considering how the individual saving and consumption decision changes, as soon as capitalistic utility is diminished.

3.2.1.2 Special case – optimal bequest decision under estate taxation

A tax on wealth transfers implicitly causes the threshold level a to increase. Hence, a higher gross bequest is needed in order to be able to gain utility from the fortune passed on to following generations. However, the utility derived from wealth holdings during lifetime remains unaffected. Figure 3.3 depicts the effect on consumption and savings with the introduction of a tax on bequest.

The actual consumption function is given by the minimum of the 45-degree line and the optimal consumption function, in which bequests are not constrained to be positive. The intersection labeled $\widetilde{w}$ identifies the level of lifetime wealth at which consumers begin to leave positive bequests. The introduction of a bequest tax shifts the intersect point to the right. The new required wealth level from which parents begin to save and to bequeath, $\widetilde{w}_{\tau^b}$, is substantially higher and increasing with the tax rate.

Figure 3.3: Consumption and savings decision with τ^b

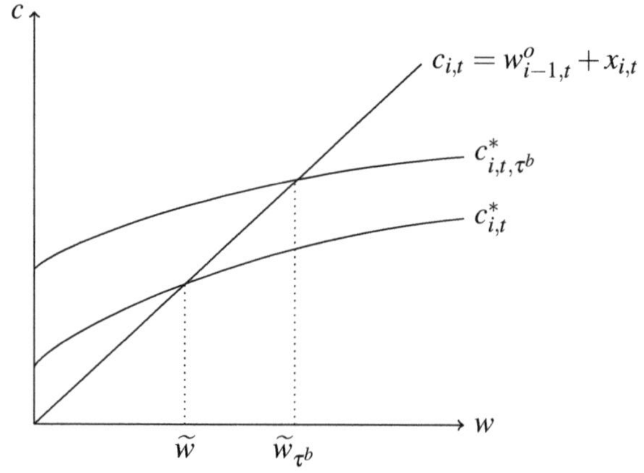

Source: Following Carroll (1998).

Hence, when wanting to analyze the effects of a wealth transfer tax introduction, three categories of individuals within the parents' generation have to be differentiated.

- Individuals with permanent lifetime income *below* $\widetilde{w}$, due to the no-borrowing constraint will never leave bequests neither when wealth transfers are untaxed nor when bequests are taxed.

- Individuals exhibiting wealth *above* $\widetilde{w}_{\tau^b}$, however, will always leave bequests, even when exposed to an estate tax. This can be argued by the existence of a strong 'capitalist spirit' which generates utility from wealth holding that is sufficiently high to compensate the utility losses induced by wealth transfer taxation.

- Individuals with lifetime wealth *between* $\widetilde{w}$ and $\widetilde{w}_{\tau^b}$ would leave bequests as long as transfers to descendants remain untaxed, but will become life-cycle savers under an estate tax. Here the 'capitalist spirit' is crowded out by wealth transfer taxation.

At first glance it appears the third category is most affected by wealth transfer taxation. However, at any level of lifetime income above the threshold a, the size of bequests left to the future generation is reduced by the amount equalizing the gap between the two consumption curves. This gap becomes wider the higher the wealth transfer tax rates.[51] Since individuals are assumed to be rational and forward-looking, they optimally determine their consumption and savings over lifetime. Anticipating future wealth transfers will be taxed, they adjust consumption and saving decisions in both periods. Thus, receiving the following proposition.

Proposition 2. *Let $\tau^b > 0$, then the behavioral changes concerning the optimum saving decision in the last period $w^{o,*}_{i,t}$ induced by taxation, can be determined as*

$$\frac{\partial w^{o,*}_{i,t,\tau^b}}{\partial \tau^b} \begin{cases} = & -\left(\frac{\partial c^{y,*}_{i,t,\tau^b}}{\partial \tau^b} + \frac{\partial c^{o,*}_{i,t,\tau^b}}{\partial \tau^b}\right) & \text{if } w^*_{i,t} \geq \widetilde{w}_{\tau^b}, \\ > & -\left(\frac{\partial c^{y,*}_{i,t,\tau^b}}{\partial \tau^b} + \frac{\partial c^{o,*}_{i,t,\tau^b}}{\partial \tau^b}\right) \text{ but} \leq 0 & \text{if } \widetilde{w} \leq w^*_{i,t} < \widetilde{w}_{\tau^b}, \\ = & 0 & \text{if } w^*_{i,t} < \widetilde{w}. \end{cases} \tag{3.10}$$

Proof. Since w^* is defined as the residual of wealth holding minus the optimal consumption level according to (3.7) and (3.8), it can be written as

$$w^{o,*}_{i,t} = w^{y}_{i,t} - c^{o,*}_{i,t} \quad \text{and} \quad w^{y,*}_{i,t} = w^{o}_{i,t-1} + x_{i,t} - c^{y,*}_{i,t}. \tag{3.11}$$

When introducing a tax on bequests (3.7) modifies to

$$c^{o,*}_{i,t,\tau^b} = \frac{(a + w^{y}_{i,t})(1+\sigma)}{1+\sigma+\gamma(2+\sigma-\tau^b)}. \tag{3.7'}$$

Applying the modified optimal consumption level (3.7') to (3.8) it holds

$$c^{y,*}_{i,t,\tau^b} = \frac{(a + w^{o}_{i,t-1} + x_{i,t})(1+\sigma)^2}{(1+\sigma)(2+\gamma+\sigma+\sigma\gamma)+\gamma(-2+\sigma-\tau^b)}. \tag{3.8'}$$

Combining (3.11), (3.7'), and (3.8'), the tax induced changes in the end of life's wealth can be calculated by

$$\frac{\partial w^{o,*}_{i,t,\tau^b}}{\partial \tau^b} = -\frac{\partial c^{y,*}_{i,t,\tau^b}}{\partial \tau^b} - \frac{\partial c^{o,*}_{i,t,\tau^b}}{\partial \tau^b}. \tag{3.12}$$

[51] In order to judge the aggregate effect of a bequest tax by extending this model to n agents, I would need to make assumptions on the distribution of individuals across these different levels of income. If most of the parent generation belong to the first group, an estate tax may have little effect on the consumption and saving decisions. If, however, among the benefactors (capitalists) most bequests will be created within the third category ($\widetilde{w}$<w<$\widetilde{w}_{\tau^b}$), then the taxation of wealth transfers can nearly reduce wealth transfers to zero, which also implies that no tax revenues are generated.

Due to the no-borrowing constraint this only holds true if $w^*_{i,t} > \widetilde{w}_{\tau^b}$. In all other cases the reduction of wealth holding is lower. For all individuals with $\widetilde{w}_{\tau^b} > w^*_{i,t} > \widetilde{w}$ it shows that wealth is reduced and consumption equivalently increased until the no-borrowing constraint binds.

$$c^{y,*}_{i,t,\tau^b} + c^{o,*}_{i,t,\tau^b} \leq w^o_{i,t-1} + x_{i,t},$$

With $w^*_{i,t} < \widetilde{w}$ individuals do not reveal any behavioral changes, given that they would not even hold wealth without an estate tax. In this case it reveals

$$w^o_{i,t-1} + x_{i,t} - (c^y_{i,t} + c^o_{i,t}) = 0, \quad \text{and it follows} \quad \frac{\partial w^{o,*}_{i,t}}{\partial \tau^b} = 0. \quad \blacksquare$$

The distortive effect on savings and hence on wealth transfers, induced by an estate tax, is larger the higher the tax rate τ^b, the higher the wealth threshold level a and the lower the 'capitalist spirit', determined by γ. The intensity of these behavioral changes can be shown in the following numerical example.

Example 3.2. Given the two dynasties H, L analog to Example 3.1, and let the tax rates τ^b on bequests vary. Since low-able individuals are life-cycle savers, irrespective of a bequest tax, they will never leave bequests to descendants. Therefore, they are excluded from this numerical example.

As can be taken from Table 3.2 there are three observations to be made.

- The introduction of τ^b causes high-able individuals, receiving a permanent lifetime income above the threshold level a, to consume more and thus save less for future generations. This effect increases with τ^b.

- The higher the wealth threshold a and the lower the capital spirit γ the stronger the distortive tax effects.

- If estate tax rates are too high (e.g. an almost confiscatory tax of $\tau^b = 0.99$), taxation might even reduce the optimal amount of terminal wealth in such way that it falls below the threshold level a. In this case, the 'capitalist spirit' is crowded out. The lower γ and the higher a the sooner this effect is released, so that at some critical tax rate τ^b even the high-able individual cannot generate utility by passing wealth into the future as well as by holding wealth during lifetime (cells marked gray).

Table 3.2: Exemplary optimal bequest decision under wealth transfer taxation

	τ^b	γ	$c^{y,*}_{H,t}$	$w^{y,*}_{H,t}$	$c^{o,*}_{H,t}$	$w^{o,*}_{H,t}$	$\frac{\partial w^{o,*}_{H,t,\tau^b}}{\partial \tau^b} / w^{o,*}_{H,t}$
$a=5$	0	1.1	5.0831	14.9169	6.4247	8.4922	
		1.5	4.1580	15.8420	5.3944	10.4476	
	0.2	1.1	5.2783	14.7217	6.8006	7.9211	-0.0672
		1.5	4.3369	15.6631	5.7543	9.9088	-0.0515
	0.4	1.1	5.4890	14.5110	7.2260	7.2850	-0.1421
		1.5	4.5318	15.4682	6.1685	9.2997	-0.1099
	0.99	1.1	6.2217	13.7783	8.997	4.7813	-0.4369
		1.5	5.2245	14.7755	7.8672	6.9083	-0.3388
$a=7$	0	1.1	5.4898	14.5102	6.9388	7.5714	
		1.5	4.4907	15.5093	5.8259	9.6834	
	0.2	1.1	5.7006	14.2994	7.3446	6.9548	-0.1128
		1.5	4.6839	15.3161	6.2146	9.1015	-0.0601
	0.4	1.1	5.9281	14.0719	7.8044	6.2675	-0.1722
		1.5	4.8943	15.1057	6.6619	8.4438	-0.1280
	0.99	1.1	6.7195	13.2805	9.6116	3.6689	-0.5154
		1.5	5.6425	14.3575	8.4967	5.5608	-0.4257

As a result, the optimum decision process of a capitalistic individual is revealed to be determined by two parameters: the *degree of 'capitalist spirit'* and the *level of wealth threshold* required to gain utility from lifetime savings as well as from terminal wealth. It holds that the more intense the 'capitalist spirit' the higher are savings and bequests. The imposition of a wealth transfer tax leads to a reduction of capitalistic savings. These distortions, however, are smaller the higher this wealth creating ambition. This implies, individuals attaching great importance to the survival of their wealth even beyond death, to reveal smaller behavioral changes. Contrasting, it can be shown the higher the wealth threshold level the smaller are savings and bequests. Since capitalistic savings become less valuable with an increase in the required minimum wealth level, individuals, if at all, solely save smaller shares of their permanent savings for capitalistic reasons. The introduction of a tax on bequests induces capitalistic savings to become even less valuable. This reveals that the higher the required amount to undertake capitalistic savings the more sensitive individuals are to wealth transfer taxation.

3.2.2 Social welfare

In order to analyze not only individual but also social effects of wealth transfer taxation, I now integrate social welfare considerations of a benevolent government imposing a *non-linear* income tax and a *linear* tax on bequest. The parents' indirect utility can be defined according to (3.1)

$$v_{i,t}(x_{i,t}, e_{i,t}, w^o_{i,t-1}, \tau^b) \equiv$$
$$max\{U_{i,t}(c^y_{i,t}, c^o_{i,t}, w^y_{i,t}, w^o_{i,t}, w^{o,\tau^b}_{i,t}, l) \mid c^y_{i,t} + c^o_{i,t} \leq x_{i,t} + w^o_{i,t-1}\}$$

For the children's generation it applies

$$v_{i,t+1}(x_{i,t+1}, e_{i,t+1}, w^o_{i,t}, \tau^b) \equiv$$
$$max\{U_{i,t}(c^y_{i,t+1}, c^o_{i,t+1}, l) \mid c^y_{i,t+1} + c^o_{i,t+1} \leq x^y_{i,t+1} + w^{o,\tau^b}_{i,t}\}$$

The maximized utility of both generations is increasing in the individual net income and the initial endowments transferred from the previous generation. Higher values of these variables lead to higher consumption and higher saving rates in both periods.

To begin with, the tax on bequests is set fixed at $\tau^b = 0$, and the government is considered to impose an optimal non-linear income tax with the objective to maximize the welfare of both dynasties as well as generations. A non-linear income tax enables the government to apply different tax parameters on different types of individuals and therewith to redistribute income from high-able to low-able individuals. This, however, might create an incentive for the former to avoid the tax burden by adjusting labor earnings to that of the low-able individual. Hence, to make the individuals voluntarily reveal their productivity type, the government has to include a revelation mechanism.

In this model, setting a non-linear income tax is equivalent to determining two bundles $(x_{L,t}, e_{L,t}), (x_{H,t}, e_{H,t})$ – implying net and gross labor earnings of both low-able and high-able individuals – subject to a self-selection constraint and a resource constraint. Even though earnings and wealth are supposed to be positively correlated, the government is assumed not to use its information on individual's initial wealth. Thus, instead of applying a differentiated lump-sum tax, the government applies a schedular tax system, levying income and bequests independently.[52] According to Mirrlees (1971) an optimal non-linear income tax system is then defined by

$$\max_{\{x_{i,t},e_{i,t}\},i=L,H} \sum_{i=L,H} q_i v_{i,t}(\cdot) + \alpha \sum_{i=L,H} q_i v_{i,t+1}(\cdot), \tag{3.13}$$

$$\text{s.t.} \quad v_{H,t}(x_{H,t}, e_{H,t}, w^o_{H,t-1}, \tau^b) \geq v^L_{H,t}(x_{L,t}, e_{L,t}, w^o_{H,t-1}, \tau^b), \tag{3.14}$$

$$(e_{H,t} - x_{H,t}) + (e_{L,t} - x_{L,t}) + \tau^b(w^o_{H,t} + w^o_{L,t}) \geq g. \tag{3.15}$$

with (3.14) as the self-selection constraint and (3.15) as the government budget constraint. $v^L_{H,t}$ denotes high-able individuals mimicking low-able ones and g the required government revenues.[53]

The social planner is assumed to weight the individual utility according to $q_L > q_H$, such that downward redistribution from high-wage to low-wage individuals is desired. The self-selection constraint, therewith, is solely binding for the rich individuals. The factor $\alpha > 0$ incorporates the descendants' welfare – which is not included in the parents' welfare function neither with a life-cycle nor with a capitalistic motive – into the governments' objective. Given gross income e_H, e_L being exogenous, a variation in net income reveals the effects of a change in non-linear income tax rates. Thus, the first order conditions of the above maximization problem with respect to $x_{L,t}$ and $x_{H,t}$ read

$$x_{L,t}: \; q_L \frac{\partial v_{L,t}}{\partial x_{L,t}} + \alpha q_L \frac{\partial v_{L,t+1}}{\partial x_{L,t}} - \mu \frac{\partial v^L_{H,t}}{\partial x_{L,t}} - \lambda = 0, \tag{3.16}$$

$$x_{H,t}: \; q_H \frac{\partial v_{H,t}}{\partial x_{H,t}} + \alpha q_H \frac{\partial v_{H,t+1}}{\partial x_{H,t}} + \mu \frac{\partial v_{H,t}}{\partial x_{H,t}} - \lambda = 0. \tag{3.17}$$

with μ and λ denoting the Lagrange multipliers for (3.14) and (3.15) respectively. Both multipliers are strictly positive.[54] These first order conditions, together with

[52] This is in accordance with actual behavior of tax authorities, which might be based on the fact that in reality the relation of earnings and inherited wealth is – at least partly – stochastic.

[53] Following Bohn (1991) current and future government spending is held constant, i.e. exogenous. The assumption of such fixed revenue requirement is common in the tax avoidance literature, e.g. Yitzhaki and Slemrod (1991), or Sandmo (2005). To analyze social welfare changes induced by the introduction of an estate tax, incorporating both generations and dynasties, we likewise suppose governmental revenue requirements to be constant over time.

[54] $\mu > 0$ implies that the self-selection constraint is binding. If it were not, the government could implement a first best tax system. However, it is obvious to show that this is not incentive compatible and thus not consistent with the self-selection constraint.

the self-selection constraint and the government's budget constraint, implicitly define an optimal non-linear tax system which will be denoted as $G^*(\tau^b)$. Hence, the question arises, whether and how an additional tax on bequests affects social welfare. Differentiation of G^* with respect to τ^b reveals the following proposition.

Proposition 3. *Let the government implement an optimal non-linear income tax system. Then the introduction of a tax on wealth transfers produces the following welfare effect*

$$\left.\frac{\partial G^*}{\partial \tau^b}\right|_{\tau^b=0} = \alpha \sum_{i=L,H} q_i\left(\frac{\partial v_{i,t+1}}{\partial \tau^b}\right) + \mu\left(\frac{\partial v_{H,t}^{o,L}}{\partial x_{L,t}}(w_{H,t}^{o,L} - w_{L,t}^{o})\right). \tag{3.18}$$

While the first term – describing the tax-induced distortions in the children's generation – is negative, the second term – indicating the redistributive effect in the parents' generation – is positive. If initial endowments were homogeneous, $w_{H,t}^{o,L} = w_{L,t}^{o}$, the effect on the self-selection constraint would be zero and the overall social welfare effect would hence be negative.[55] *But, due to the assumption that initial wealth of high- and low-able individuals differs, the overall effect in the present setting is ambiguous, depending on whether the first or the second term prevails.*

Proof. Using the Envelope Theorem, we generate the optimum value function $G^*(\tau^b)$ at $\tau^b = 0$

$$\frac{\partial G^*}{\partial \tau^b} = \sum_{i=L,H} q_i\left(\frac{\partial v_{i,t}}{\partial \tau^b} + \alpha\frac{\partial v_{i,t+1}}{\partial \tau^b}\right) + \mu\left(\frac{\partial v_{H,t}}{\partial \tau^b} - \frac{\partial v_{H,t}^{L}}{\partial \tau^b}\right) + \lambda(w_{L,t}^{o} + w_{H,t}^{o}). \tag{3.19}$$

Substituting $\frac{\partial v_{i,t}}{\partial \tau^b}$ using Roy's Identity $\frac{\partial v_{i,t}}{\partial \tau^b} = -w_{i,t}^{o}\frac{\partial v_{i,t}}{\partial x_{i,t}}$ and the first order conditions multiplied with $w_{L,t}^{o}$ and $w_{H,t}^{o}$ respectively

$$q_L\frac{\partial v_{L,t}}{\partial \tau^b} = w_{L,t}^{o}\alpha q_L\frac{\partial v_{L,t+1}}{\partial x_{L,t}} - w_{L,t}^{o}\mu\frac{\partial v_{H,t}^{L}}{\partial x_{L,t}} - \lambda w_{L,t}^{o},$$

$$q_H\frac{\partial v_{H,t}}{\partial \tau^b} = w_{H,t}^{o}\alpha q_H\frac{\partial v_{H,t+1}}{\partial x_{H,t}} + w_{H,t}^{o}\mu\frac{\partial v_{H,t}}{\partial x_{H,t}} - \lambda w_{H,t}^{o}.$$

[55] This result is obviously related to the findings of Atkinson and Stiglitz (1980), who have shown that an optimal non-linear income tax is sufficient in order to redistribute within a generation. Their considerations lead to the result that an additional taxation of wealth transfers would have a negative welfare effect.

This leads to

$$\frac{\partial G^*}{\partial \tau^b} = \alpha \sum_{i=L,H} q_i(\frac{\partial v_{i,t+1}}{\partial x_{i,t}} + \frac{\partial v_{i,t+1}}{\partial \tau^b}) + \mu(\frac{\partial v^L_{H,t}}{\partial x_{L,t}}(w^L_{H,t} - w_{L,t})).$$

When applying the Slutsky-equation it holds

$$\left.\frac{\partial G^*}{\partial \tau^b}\right|_{\tau^b=0} = \alpha \sum_{i=L,H} q_i(\frac{\partial v_{i,t+1}}{\partial \tau^b}) + \mu(\frac{\partial v^L_{H,t}}{\partial x_{L,t}}(w^L_{H,t} - w_{L,t})). \quad \blacksquare$$

Since the high-able individual is endowed with more initial wealth, she will, even when mimicking, leave more bequests to her descendant than the low-able individual does. Therefore, it holds $w^L_{H,t} > w_{L,t}$. If an estate tax is introduced, the government is able to increase tax revenues by $\Delta\tau^b(w^o_{H,t} + w^o_{L,t})$. This allows for the possibility to compensate the individuals of the parents' generation with an equivalent reduction in income tax $\Delta\tau^b w^o_{i,t} = \Delta x_{i,t}$. Given that $w^o_{H,t} > w^o_{L,t}$, the compensation must be higher for high-able individuals $\Delta x_{H,t} > \Delta x_{L,t}$. Hence, the self-selection constraint is relaxed, due to the fact that the opportunity to mimic becomes less attractive for the high-able individual. By facilitating the government to further redistribute via the income tax the taxation on wealth transfers elicits a positive welfare effect. However, an additional welfare-decreasing negative price effect affects the descendants' generation, whose initial inheritances are reduced by wealth transfer taxation and thus would rather call for a subsidy on bequests.

As a result, the impact of wealth transfer taxation on social welfare under the 'capitalist spirit' assumption decisively depends on the difference in initial wealth levels and on the parameter α, describing the social rate of discounting the welfare of future generations.[56] If wealth inequality is zero, as in Atkinson and Stiglitz (1980), or infinitesimal small the positive redistributive effect has virtually no impact, so that the negative distortive effect prevails. However, with the existence of a 'capitalist spirit', which implicitly presumes a sizable difference in initial wealth of high-able and low-able individuals, the redistributive effect becomes clearly evident. Hence, this positive impact induced by the estate tax might justify its existence. In the optimum, the estate tax rate should be set to balance both, the distortive and the redistributive effect, best possibly.

Nonetheless, high estate tax rates generally will be avoided by the individuals involved. For the high-able individual following a 'capitalist spirit' the formation of a charitable foundation therein provides a preferable instrument to prevent own

[56] If α is set to zero the estate tax would only have a positive redistributive effect.

wealth from being taxed.[57] In order to analyze this effect, I allow for the existence of charitable foundation in the following section.

3.3 The existence of self-governed foundations

The present model has been limited, so far, to only one possibility of preserving the own fortune beyond death – via bequests to descendants. I now allow for the existence of own foundations which can perfectly replace the dynasty in the continuation process of own wealth in the future. Hence, the individual has to choose not only which fraction of the fortune to transfer, but also how to allocate the fortune between descendants and the own foundation.[58] Contrary to passing wealth on to the own dynasty, which is intended to continue the will of their ancestors free of costs, the foundation is assumed to require a specific capital stock d^f to be instituted and proportional costs k^f to be run. These costs obviously reduce the utility gained from wealth holding.

Most societies grant philanthropists tax deductibility for donations and charitable bequests. Foundations set up by an individual, a family, or a group of individuals can pursue public or private interests. Whereas charitable foundations enjoy tax shelter, a family foundation which solely serves private interest is taxed like any other legal entity.[59]

In order to incorporate the idea of a tax privilege into this model, I allow for charitable foundations only and assume the government to exempt these foundations from the estate tax. The rate of return r_t^f generated within the foundation is supposed to accrue into public revenues, such that the budget constraint in (3.15) changes to

$$(e_{H,t} - x_{H,t}) + (e_{L,t} - x_{L,t}) + \tau^b (w_{H,t}^o + w_{L,t}^o) \geq g_t - r_t^f (w_{i,t}^{o,f}(P_{i,t})), \qquad (3.20)$$

[57]Empirical evidence shows that the taxation of wealth transfers reduces the price for charitable bequests and hence causes strong incentive effects to avoid taxation by charitable giving. See Bakija, Gale and Slemrod (2003).

[58]I will show that given the simple model, there will only be all-or-nothing decisions. Capitalists maximize their utility either by bequeathing the entire fortune to the descendants or to the foundation.

[59]Foundations may have a diversity of forms and may follow different regulations. These depend on the jurisdiction in which they are created. In most countries solely charitable organizations are characterized as foundations, whereas in some others they differentiate between foundations following public interests (charity) and private interests. Generally, charities receive tax shelter in almost all countries.

with $w^{o,f}$ describing the amount of wealth inherited to the charitable foundation. This amount depends on $P_{i,t}$, describing the price of charitable contributions relative to the price for bequests to the own family

$$P_{i,t} = \frac{(w^o_{i,t} + d^f)/(1 - k^f)}{(w^o_{i,t} + a)/(1 - \tau^b)}.$$

The taxation of dynastic bequests reduces the price for charitable transfers to the foundation and increases the amount of charitable bequests. Thereby, it generates additional revenues for the government, so that the national budget is relaxed, offering the possibility to cut taxes or to increase redistribution. Both aspects enhance social welfare.[60]

Given that a capitalist is solely interested in seeing her fortune continued beyond own death, a charitable foundation, in which the lifework and the testator's name are maintained, offers a perfect and tax-free alternative to pass on wealth into the future.

Let in the following the minimum capital stock needed to form a foundation d^f be strictly larger than the wealth threshold level a. Thus, in equilibrium no foundation exists, if $\tau^b = 0$, or if $k^f \geq \tau^b$, and the results of Section 3.2 remain. However, this changes as soon as the costs to run the foundation k^f are lower than the estate tax rate τ^b. Then, all capitalists with wealth holding $w^o_{i,t} > d^f$ have the opportunity to avoid estate taxation by forming an own foundation, anticipating that d^f is the minimum financial requirement to form a foundation and $d^f > a$. The new wealth threshold level, above which the individual is able to avoid taxation by installing an own charitable foundation is denoted by $\hat{w}$.

Figure 3.4 depicts that tax effects for some part of the capitalists are relaxed, when allowing for the existence of charitable foundations. Even though, facing operating costs when transferring wealth to a foundation which would not accrue when bequeathing to the descendants, these costs, nonetheless, are smaller than being taxed.

[60] With this assumption we abstract from any specific mission a foundation normally pursues by funding special interests e.g. in health care, education, culture etc.. Thereby any influence exercised by the benefactor is excluded. The return is incorporated in the public revenues without a specified appropriation.

Figure 3.4: Consumption and savings decision with τ^b and the existence of foundations

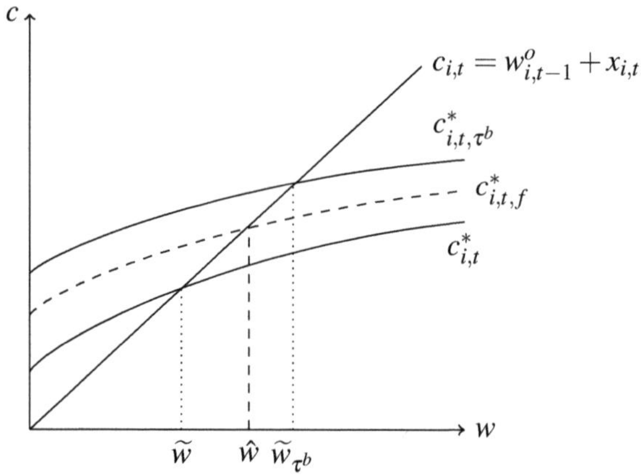

The capitalists' utility function for those decedents holding wealth above the threshold level d^f changes to

$$U_i = \frac{(c^y_{i,t})^{1-\mu}}{1-\mu} + \gamma\frac{(w^y_{i,t}+a)^{1-\phi}}{1-\phi} + \frac{(1-l_i)^{1-\mu}}{1-\mu} + \frac{\frac{(c^o_{i,t})^{1-\mu}}{1-\mu} + \gamma\frac{(w^o_{i,t}+a)^{1-\phi}}{1-\phi}}{1+\sigma} + \gamma\frac{\frac{(w^{o,f}_{i,t}+d^f)^{1-\phi}}{1-\phi}}{(1+\sigma)^2}.$$

Therefore, the findings of Section 3.2 can be revised, and by modifying Proposition 2 it holds

$$\frac{\partial w^{o,*}_{t,i,f}}{\partial \tau^b} \begin{cases} = & -\left(\frac{\partial c^{y,*}_{i,t,f}}{\partial \tau^b} + \frac{\partial c^{o,*}_{i,t,f}}{\partial \tau^b}\right) & \text{if } \; w^*_{i,t} \geq \hat{w}, \\ > & -\left(\frac{\partial c^{y,*}_{i,t,\tau^b}}{\partial \tau^b} + \frac{\partial c^{o,*}_{i,t,\tau^b}}{\partial \tau^b}\right) \text{ but } \leq 0 & \text{if } \; \widetilde{w} \leq w^*_{i,t} < \hat{w}, \\ = & 0 & \text{if } \; w^*_{i,t} < \widetilde{w}. \end{cases} \tag{3.21}$$

Capitalistic individuals with $\widetilde{w} \leq w^*_{i,t} < \hat{w}$ do not have the opportunity to avoid taxation. Their wealth holding $w^*_{i,t}$ is not big enough to afford the minimum financial requirement d^f to install a foundation, such that they are forced to become life-cycle savers.

In terms of social welfare, the existence of foundations causes a decreasing part of individual wealth to underlie taxation. Since the possibility to avoid the bequest tax is only given to the very rich, it is solely the 'poor capitalist' with wealth $\widetilde{w} \leq w^*_{i,t} < \hat{w}$ who can be charged by the government. Direct redistribution via bequest taxation, therewith, is obviously diminished or even crowded out completely.

Equivalently to Section 3.2, the optimal non-linear income tax system can thus be developed, using (3.13), (3.14), and the modified government budget constraint (3.20), revealing

$$\max_{\{x_{i,t},e_{i,t}\},i=L,H} \sum_{i=L,H} q_i v_{i,t}(\cdot) + \alpha \sum_{i=L,H} q_i v_{i,t+1}(\cdot),$$

$$\text{s.t.} \quad v_{H,t}(x_{H,t}, e_{H,t}, w^o_{H,t-1}, \tau^b) \geq v^L_{H,t}(x_{L,t}, e_{L,t}, w^o_{H,t-1}, \tau^b),$$

$$(e_{H,t} - x_{H,t}) + (e_{L,t} - x_{L,t}) + \tau^b(w^o_{H,t} + w^o_{L,t}) \geq g_t - r^f_t(w^{o,f}_{i,t}).$$

Supposing the social planner still weights the individual utility according to $q_L > q_H$, then the first order conditions (3.16) and (3.17) together with the self-selection constraint and the modified government's budget constraint implicitly define an optimal non-linear tax system denoted as $G^{*,f}(\tau^b)$. Differentiating with respect to τ^b leads to the following proposition.

Proposition 4. *The social welfare effect of estate taxation within an environment in which tax avoidance by charitable bequests is available reads*

$$\left.\frac{\partial G^{*,f}}{\partial \tau^b}\right|_{\tau^b=0} = \alpha \sum_{i=L,H} q_i\left(\frac{\partial v_{i,t+1}}{\partial \tau^b}\right) + \mu\left(\frac{\partial v^{o,L}_{H,t}}{\partial x_{L,t}}(w^{o,L}_{H,t} - w^o_{L,t})\right) + \lambda\left(r^f_t \frac{\partial w^{o,f}_{i,t}}{\partial \tau^b}\right). \tag{3.22}$$

By incorporation of charitable foundations, becoming public property at decedents' death, the introduction of a bequest tax leads to an additional positive term. This term can be described by the positive price effect on charitable bequests. Given that the first and second term have the same properties as in (3.18)*, but may vary in their intensity, the overall welfare effect remains ambiguous.*

Proof. Analog to Proposition 3, the Envelope Theorem is used to generate the optimum value function $G^{*,f}(\tau^b)$ at $\tau^b = 0$

$$\frac{\partial G^*}{\partial \tau^b} = \sum_{i=L,H} s_i\left(\frac{\partial v_{i,t}}{\partial \tau^b} + \alpha \frac{\partial v_{i,t+1}}{\partial \tau^b}\right)$$

$$+ \mu\left(\frac{\partial v_{H,t}}{\partial \tau^b} - \frac{\partial v^L_{H,t}}{\partial \tau^b}\right) + \lambda\left(w^o_{L,t} + w^o_{H,t} + r_t \frac{w^{o,f}_{i,t}}{\partial \tau^b}\right). \tag{3.23}$$

Substituting $\frac{\partial v_{i,t}}{\partial \tau^b}$ using Roy's Identity $\frac{\partial v_{i,t}}{\partial \tau^b} = -w^o_{i,t} \frac{\partial v_{i,t}}{\partial x_{i,t}}$ and the first order conditions multiplied with $w^o_{L,t}$ and $w^o_{H,t}$ respectively

$$s_L \frac{\partial v_{L,t}}{\partial \tau^b} = w^o_{L,t} \alpha q_L \frac{\partial v_{L,t+1}}{\partial x_{L,t}} - w^o_{L,t} \mu \frac{\partial v^L_{H,t}}{\partial x_{L,t}} - \lambda w^o_{L,t},$$

$$s_H \frac{\partial v_{H,t}}{\partial \tau^b} = w^o_{H,t} \alpha q_H \frac{\partial v_{H,t+1}}{\partial x_{H,t}} + w^o_{H,t} \mu \frac{\partial v_{H,t}}{\partial x_{H,t}} - \lambda w^o_{H,t}.$$

This leads to

$$\frac{\partial G^*}{\partial \tau^b} = \alpha \sum_{i=L,H} q_i \left(\frac{\partial v_{i,t+1}}{\partial x_{i,t}} + \frac{\partial v_{i,t+1}}{\partial \tau^b} \right) + \mu \left(\frac{\partial v^L_{H,t}}{\partial x_{L,t}} (w^L_{H,t} - w_{L,t}) \right) + \lambda \left(r_t \frac{w^{o,f}_{i,t}}{\partial \tau^b} \right).$$

When applying the Slutsky-equation, it reveals

$$\left. \frac{\partial G^*}{\partial \tau^b} \right|_{\tau^b=0} = \alpha \sum_{i=L,H} q_i \left(\frac{\partial v_{i,t+1}}{\partial \tau^b} \right) + \mu \left(\frac{\partial v^L_{H,t}}{\partial x_{L,t}} (w^L_{H,t} - w_{L,t}) \right) + \lambda \left(r_t \frac{w^{o,f}_{i,t}}{\partial \tau^b} \right). \quad \blacksquare$$

Hence, if the positive impact induced by the estate tax preponderates, this implies that even high estate tax rates can enhance redistribution given that rich individuals are forced to invest their fortune in charitable foundations. However, a valuation of the distortive and redistributive effects compared to Section 3.2 is unfeasible. Even though there might be positive welfare indications, based on this model one cannot assert that (excessive) taxation of wealth transfers unequivocally could have welfare increasing effects by coercing the very wealthy capitalists to form own charitable foundations.

3.4 Concluding remarks

This chapter has analyzed the individual as well as the social welfare effects of a bequest tax levied on the very rich. Given that in almost all societies big fortunes are held by a few individuals, these findings are essential, particularly, since empirical evidence has proven that the rich rather seem to follow capitalistic motivations than common family concerns. As a consequence, they are supposed to exhibit the aspiration to see their own name and lifework continued beyond death, inheriting all their wealth to those recipients able to fulfill their ambition best possibly.

With regard to *individual effects*, I have shown that an inheritance to the dynastic family becomes less attractive as soon as bequests are taxed. However, the greater the importance attached to the survival of own wealth beyond death (the larger the 'capitalist spirit') the smaller behavioral changes are. The taxation of bequests, nonetheless, induces the capitalistic benefactor to search for an alternative to maintain her wealth holding in the future. Therefore, the formation of an own charitable foundation that generally enjoys tax exemption, for example, might be regarded as a consequence of wealth transfer taxation. Raising the price for bequests, wealth transfer taxes impose an extraordinary burden on the capitalists and endanger the persistence of their fortunes, leading to a strong incentive effect on tax avoidance activities.

Respecting *social welfare consequences*, ambiguous results are observed, given that wealth transfer taxation is undesirable for the capitalist's individual utility, but at the same time enhances redistribution. Additionally to heterogeneous earning abilities, further heterogeneity of initial wealth is presumed which results from unequal wealth transfers in the past. Thereby the traditional findings of Atkinson and Stiglitz (1980) cannot be applied. In contrast, it can be shown that, due to differences in initial wealth, the taxation of wealth transfers supplementary to an non-linear income tax, induces two ambiguous effects – a *distortive* (known from the traditional literature) and a *redistributive* effect. The latter, moreover, can be supposed to be larger the stronger the differences in initial wealth. Since wealth is assumed to differ considerably in our capitalistic bequest model, considering a high-able (wealthy) and a low-able (poor) dynasty, the redistributive effect might preponderate, justifying the existence of estate taxation.[61]

The extension to charitable bequests captures the fact that excessive wealth transfer taxation, generally, will be avoided by the testators. Thus, assuming estate tax rates to be higher than the costs to run a charitable foundation, the option to bequeath to charity becomes rather attractive. Given the tax environment, 'rich' capitalists who can afford to institute a foundation, can therewith increase own utility, whereas the 'poor' capitalists are exposed to full estate taxation. Resulting in solely the very rich having the best opportunities for tax planning activities. However, the testator's decision to inherit the own fortune to charity also influences social welfare. Since, on the one hand, the foundation is assumed to become public property at the benefactor's death, redistributive means are strengthened. On the other hand, the distortive effect on the descendant's generation concurrently increases: Poor capitalists are forced to become life-cycle savers, whereas the rich completely shift their bequests to their own foundation – both reducing dynastic bequests to zero. Whichever effect prevails is undetermined, so that one cannot

[61] Even though I did not study the optimal value of an inheritance tax, it is obvious that the equilibrium tax rate should balance both effects at the best.

assess if forcing the wealthy to form an own charitable foundation enhances social welfare.

As a result, the 'capitalist spirit' has revealed to be more adequate to describe the preferences of the very wealthy than common bequest motives. On the basis of this finding, normative implications suggest that low or moderate taxes on capitalistic bequests supplementary to labor income taxation might be able to increase social welfare. Nonetheless, with imposing taxes on personal wealth, the social planer, constantly has to bear in mind tax avoidance schemes of the affected. Except for charitable foundations, these were omitted in the previous analysis. Especially in regard to very wealthy individuals, tax avoidance possibilities, however, can be supposed to be manifold.

4 Political-economic aspects of taxing capitalistic bequests

"There's only one kind of tax that would please everybody - one that nobody but the other guy has to pay."

Earl Wilson

In modern democracies generally the principle of *one man – one vote* holds. Whereas the right to vote is distributed equally within society, income and especially wealth are not, such that the median voter falls short of the average. Under these circumstances one might suppose the majority of voters to impose a tax system which redistributes all income and wealth to the mean. Following Robin Hood "Rob the rich – Give to the poor." the winning coalition of the poorest fifty percent could theoretically make all its members better off by confiscatory taxation. But, having a closer look at most democracies the question arises why, nonetheless, such great wealth inequality still exists.

Various efforts to explain this question can be found in literature. Meltzer and Richard (1981) argue that expropriating the rich reduces work incentives and thereby limits redistribution. Therefore, the median voter, maximizing her personal income as the sum of wage and welfare payments, will not vote for confiscatory taxes. Slemrod (2001) and Traxler (2009) similarly argue that if the rich have the opportunity to avoid taxation, extensive redistribution becomes unattainable. Breyer and Ursprung (1998) further suppose that the rich will escape expropriation by being economically powerful. They analyze whether these wealthy individuals are in a position to forge a majority coalition with the middle class to avoid redistribution to the mean, and whether they might be able to influence the politically powerful by holding out the prospect of financial support (e.g. in election campaigns).

Since inherited wealth commonly is regarded as an unjustified advantage for some wealthy individuals at the expense of others, taxation of these wealth transfers is considered to ensure the equality of opportunities. In this chapter I want to investigate, whether the political outcome in a direct democracy regarding the taxation of capitalistic bequests produces the same result as gained in an optimal tax system with social welfare considerations, analyzed in Chapter 3.

There is little theoretical and empirical literature on the political economy of intergenerational wealth transfers. Solely Aura (2004) observes that in a median-voter framework with homogeneous agents and under the absence of policy commitment, wealth transfers are taxed too heavily compared to the optimum of the social planner. This is due to the fact that with positive population growth always the young voter decides upon the tax rates, favoring low taxes on labor income and high taxes on estates. In an heterogeneous society Renström (1996) analyzes the voting behavior of agents differing in age, productivity, and bequest motives with regard to tax rates on consumption, labor, and capital income. He finds that tax levels are subject to the median bequest motive. Therefore the voting outcome, and hence the entire fiscal policy, depends on the distribution of preferences in society. In a related approach Huffman (1996) observes that wealth distribution influences agent's voting behavior on labor and capital income tax levels and vice versa. Likewise, Hammar, Jagers and Nordblom (2006) show in an empirical study that support for an abolishment or decrease in estate tax rates is more likely among the old and among high income groups.[62] Similarly Tabellini (1991), considering intergenerational redistribution by public debt, shows that within a median-voter model debt is completely repaid even though it favors the rich. This is due to the fact that repudiation would have negative redistributive consequences, causing a majority to prefer repaying the debt.

In order to develop the politically viable level of wealth transfer taxation applied on capitalistic bequests, I consider a model with agents being heterogeneous in age and wealth. As the normative equilibrium – evolved in Chapter 3 – indicates, a taxation of capitalistic wealth transfers might be economically justifiable as long as the redistributive effect outweighs the distortive effect. A bequest tax set at a low rate might hence be optimal even in the long run. The political outcome I analyze in the following in contrast proposes at least a moderate tax on estates. My approach is to reveal why there is such conflict between the voting outcome and the normative implications. I therefore model two voting scenarios which are analyzed by use of numerical examples. Initially, I examine individual's preferences according to the alternative taxation of bequests versus labor income. Then, I illustrate another case where bequest taxation is used to generate additional revenues for redistributive public pensions. The numerical findings reveal that in both settings wealth heterogeneity creates a constituency to support wealth transfer taxation, which is even enlarged as soon as revenues are redistributed.

[62] Here a positive correlation of wealth with high income and age is supposed.

The chapter is organized as follows. Section 4.1 gives an overview of the politically relevant stylized facts of wealth transfer taxation. Section 4.2 provides the model and evolves the political-economic equilibrium using numerical examples. Section 4.3 discusses the effects on the political outcome when the underlying parameters change. Therein I analyze the influence of the economic power of the rich, society's aging and incomplete policy commitment. Section 4.4 finally concludes.

4.1 Stylized facts

The idea to study the political economic equilibrium of a tax on capitalistic wealth transfers is based on the fact that even though the majority of most societies is unaffected by estate taxation, nevertheless, a confiscatory tax on wealth transfers does not exist. Within the last decades, bequest tax revenues have been rather declining in many OECD countries. Some have even abolished their bequest tax completely, so that the importance of wealth transfer taxes in terms of total revenues seems to be constantly diminishing.[63]

Bertocchi (2007) argues that this decremented importance of wealth transfer taxes, on the one hand, can be originated in the overall declining wealth inequality during the twentieth century. On the other hand, she states that, due to changes in wealth composition, differential rates of tax avoidance have evolved. Wealth has been shifted from land to capital ownership, and hence taxation is much easier to avoid. In this regard, the intensity of wealth taxes, moreover, would reflect the degree of democracy and the political power of the elites.

Looking at current wealth transfer tax policies in almost all OECD countries, one can observe that all individuals being subject to unlimited taxation are entitled – in some countries even vast – tax exemptions for bequests.[64]

As empirical literature on the example of *Germany* exhibits, the majority of wealth transfers is given to spouses and own children with an average wealth transfer amount of about 250,000 euros. Accounting for exemptions given to the closest relative, one can presume that only a small part of the German society underlies inheritance taxation at all (Figure 4.2; marked dark gray).[65]

Consequently, German inheritance tax directly affects only a small economic elite. Translated into figures, in 2008 about 190,000 wealth transfers were made. Solely 8,970 of these inheritances were larger than the exemptions credited to

[63] See Chapter 5.3.
[64] A detailed overview is given in Chapter 5.1.
[65] This is consistent with the empirical findings. See Statistisches Bundesamt (2010).

Figure 4.1: Evolution of bequest taxes as share of total revenues for selected OECD countries

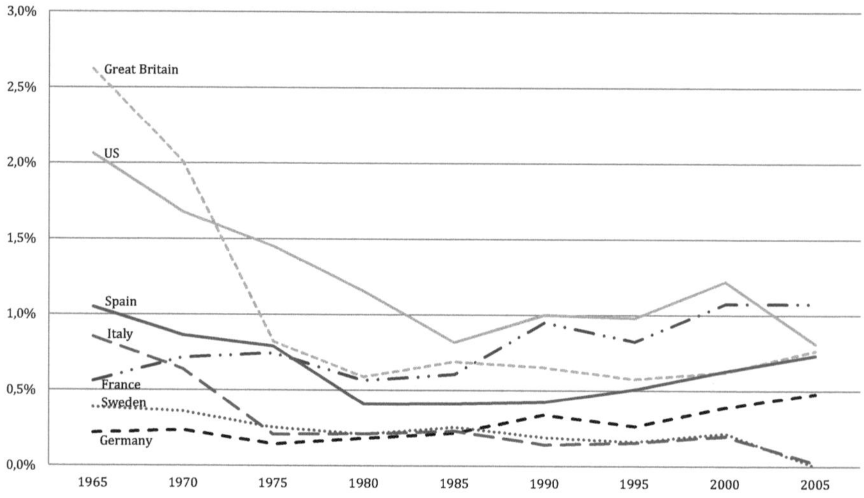

Source: Revenue Statistics 1965-2007, OECD (2009); own illustration.

spouses and children.[66] Thus, most of the inheritance tax is assessed on less than 5% of the annual heirs and is therefore paid mainly on the estates of the super-rich. This picture is quite similar in almost all OECD countries, so that in general the very wealthy individuals, as major taxpayer's, obviously would benefit most from the abolition of wealth transfer taxes. Tax avoidance behavior and economic power of the very rich could therefore have a great impact on tax policy design.

I want to show in the following that within heterogeneous societies confiscatory taxation of estates is politically nonviable under majority rule. Even though children outnumber parents as well as the poor outnumber the rich, not more than a moderate tax on wealth transfers will be preferred by a majority of voters.

[66] See Statistisches Bundesamt (2010).

Figure 4.2: Number of inheritances according to value in Germany 2008

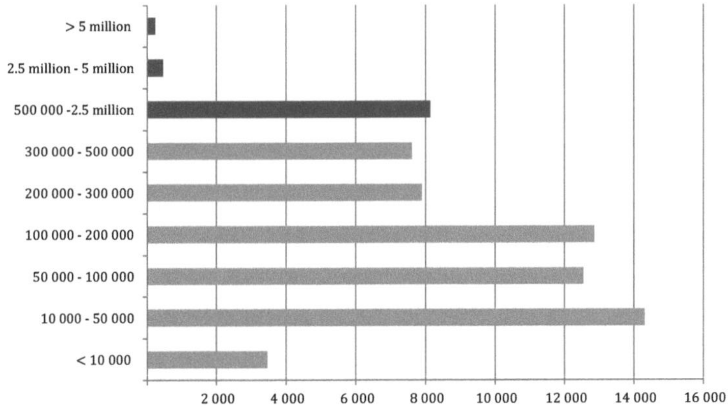

Source: Wealth Transfer Statistics, Statistisches Bundesamt (2010); own illustration.

4.2 The Model

Consider an economy with an odd number of individuals. These are divided into two generations – the parents, living for one period only and the children born in t, living for two periods. Thereby I generate a simple overlapping generation model in which I focus on solely one generation overlap to describe the voting process in society.[67] The old generation consists further of m parents, each of them has $1+n$ children, where $n \gtreqless 0$ describes the rate of population growth. I assume no family link between the generations to exist. Wealthy parents, above a critical wealth threshold, are assumed to follow a 'capitalist spirit' bequest motive, gaining additional utility by wealth holding while alive and by the survival of their wealth beyond death.[68] All other parents as well as the entire children's generation are assumed to be pure life-cycle savers, smoothing consumption over time.

[67] In order to analyze voting behavior and political majorities, the setting of this model differs from that used to identify the normative equilibrium. Instead of two generations living for two periods each, I now assume the economy to start with two generations simultaneously alive – so that the old individuals live one period only and the young survive until economy ends in $t+1$. Using this setting, solely one voting process is held, in which the old are entirely detached from any decision on labor and the young have to incorporate current and future tax effects.

[68] These characteristics are analyzed in detail in Chapter 3.

Thus in period t, the ith parent and child maximize

$$U_{i,t-1}(c,w) = u(c^o_{i,t-1}) + \gamma w^o_{i,t-1} + \gamma \frac{w^o_{i,t-1}(1-\tau^b_{t+1})}{(1+\sigma)}, \tag{4.1}$$

$$U_{i,t}(c) = u(c^y_{i,t}) + \frac{c^o_{i,t}}{1+\sigma}. \tag{4.2}$$

$u(\cdot)$ is strictly concave, strictly increasing, and twice continuously differentiable. I denote σ the time preference rate and $\gamma \geq 0$ the degree of the capitalist spirit determining the emphasis given to the wealth term.[69] The individual specific variables c and w describe consumption and wealth holding, respectively. Superscripts denote current age (young and old), and subscripts mark the individual's period of birth. The net wealth transferred from the old to the next generation is denoted by $w^o(1-\tau^b_{t+1})$ with τ^b_{t+1} indicating second period estate tax.

Figure 4.3: Time path of the model

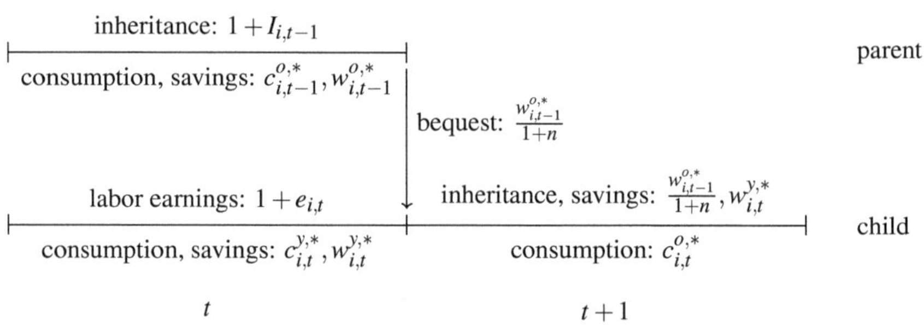

At the beginning of period t the old individual inherits $1+I_{i,t-1}$ units of wealth. The individual-specific variable $I_{i,t-1}$ is strictly positive and distributed according to a known distribution $H(\cdot)$, with mean I_{t-1}, median $I_{M,t-1} < I_{t-1}$ and bounded support $[\underline{I}, \overline{I}]$ in the interval [0,1]. These inheritances are used to finance present consumption as well as savings, which are bequeathed to the young generation at the end of the first period. The young individual earns a positive income $1+e_{i_t}$ in her first period of life, by which she funds present consumption and savings for old-age. The individual-specific labor income e_{i_t}, which can be denoted as innate ability, is distributed with a known distribution $G(\cdot)$, with mean e_t, median

[69] With $\gamma = 0$ the model reduces to a standard precautionary saving's model, which occurs with wealth holding below the aforementioned critical threshold.

$e_{M,t} < e_t$ and bounded support $[\underline{e}, \overline{e}]$ in the interval [0,1]. To present the main results, I further assume that, given the individual specific innate earning ability, labor is supplied inelastically by the young generation.[70]

The government budget requirements g are obtained by taxes on labor earnings τ_t^l and on inheritances τ_t^b in the first period. These taxes are levied on the individual specific shares of wealth and income only. Thus in period t each individual – young and old – enjoys a tax-exempt amount of one, above which additional labor income and wealth is taxed proportionally.[71] Since the old individuals die after one period, second period government budget has to be funded by wealth transfer taxes τ_{t+1}^b only. These are levied on the entire wealth bequeathed, without any tax allowances. Considering the tax rates, the budget constraints of parents and children in t hold, respectively

$$c_{i,t-1}^o = 1 + I_{i,t-1}(1 - \tau_t^b) - w_{i,t-1}^o, \tag{4.3}$$

$$c_{i,t}^y = 1 + e_{i,t}(1 - \tau_t^l) - w_{i,t}^y. \tag{4.4}$$

Once retired children live off their savings and receive a (differing) wealth transfer from the previous generation. Hence, their budget constraint in period $t+1$ can be written as

$$c_{i,t}^o = w_{i,t}^y + \frac{w_{i,t-1}^o}{1+n}(1 - \tau_{t+1}^b). \tag{4.5}$$

Given that parents are not allowed to leave negative bequests, a non-negativity constraint has to be added. Thus, savings of the parents' generation can equivalently be determined by

$$w_{i,t-1}^o = \max(0; 1 + I_{i,t-1}(1 - \tau_t^b) - c_{i,t-1}^{o,*}), \tag{4.6}$$

with $c^{o,*}$ denoting optimal old-age consumption.

In order to determine a political-economic equilibrium three conditions have to be satisfied. First, an economic equilibrium holds, if individual economic decisions are optimal for any given policy. Additionally, the political equilibrium is reached, if the policy implemented is (weakly) preferred to any other alternative by a majority of voters in every period. Finally, rationality of individuals must be given, such that economic and political expectations are fulfilled. So as to derive the economic as well as the political equilibrium, individuals are assumed to have

[70] It can be shown that elastic labor supply does not change the qualitative results I find in the following, but they become much more complicated.

[71] This should reflect lump-sum allowances given to work force and heirs in almost all national tax regimes.

perfect information on the decision process, understand the voting structure and be able to predict tax rates as a function of today's choices.

4.2.1 Economic equilibrium

Optimal decisions of individuals in their role as economic agents can be analyzed by taking current and expected future policy as given. Under these circumstances, parents as well as children maximize their individual utility by optimizing consumption and savings over time. Using equations (4.1) and (4.3) to derive the first order condition, it is straightforward to show that the optimal amount saved by each parent in period t can be determined by

$$\frac{\partial u^o_{i,t-1}}{\partial \tau^b_t}(1+I_{i,t-1}(1-\tau^b_t)-w^o_{i,t-1}) \geq \gamma(1+\frac{1-\tau^b_{t+1}}{1+\sigma}) \tag{4.7}$$

Hence, parent's optimal economic decisions depend on both present and second period taxes levied on wealth transfers. If inequality in (4.7) is strict, the non-negativity constraint is binding. This is true for those parents receiving a low inheritance, given that for low wealth levels the marginal utility of consumption is strictly larger than the marginal utility of savings. Thus, all parents with $1+I_{i,t-1} \leq c^{o,*}_{i,t-1}$ save and bequeath a zero amount. These individuals are pure life-cycle savers. With equality, however, savings and bequests are positive, and parents accumulate and transfer wealth in accordance to present and future tax rates.

Similarly, each child optimizes his lifetime consumption according to equation (4.2) and the budget constraints (4.4) and (4.5). In period t the economic equilibrium is then determined by the first order condition

$$\frac{\partial u^y_{i,t}}{\partial \tau^b_t}(1+e_{i,t}(1-\tau^l_t)-c^o_{i,t}+\frac{w^o_{i,t-1}}{1+n}(1-\tau^b_{t+1})) \geq \frac{1}{1+\sigma}. \tag{4.8}$$

Children's optimal economic decisions in t are thus determined by present and second period tax rates levied on earnings and wealth transfers as well as by the amount bequeathed by the old generation, which itself depends on present and future bequest tax rates. Thus, for parents and children I receive the following indirect utilities, respectively

$$v_{i,t-1}(\tau^b_t,\tau^b_{t+1}) = \\ u(1+I_{i,t-1}(1-\tau^b_t)-w^{o,*}_{i,t-1})+w^{o,*}_{i,t-1}\gamma\left(1+\frac{1-\tau^b_{t+1}}{1+\sigma}\right), \tag{4.9}$$

$$v_{i,t}(\tau_t^l, \tau_{t+1}^b) =$$
$$u(1 + e_{i,t}(1 - \tau_t^l) - c_{i,t}^{o,*} + \frac{w_{i,t-1}^o}{1+n}(1 - \tau_{t+1}^b)) + \frac{c_{i,t}^{o,*}}{1+\sigma}. \quad (4.10)$$

These are to be analyzed, when it comes to vote on the bequest tax rate.

4.2.2 Political equilibrium

To be able to pursue the following analysis one feature deserves special attention. By assuming quasilinear preferences of parents and children the effect of tax distortions and hence the analysis of the political equilibrium is simplified. It implies that voter's preferences are single-peaked. Such that optimal tax policy, chosen by majority rule within a one-dimensional policy space, can be determined according to the median-voter theorem.

In doing so, I assume the government to hold a referendum on the estate tax rate at the beginning of the first period before economic decisions are made. Since I model overlapping generations, old and young individuals simultaneously vote on the tax rates, and it can be presumed that voters form coalitions along their age. However, given I further assume heterogeneity in wealth, political agents may additionally vote according to own present and future wealth holding. Thus, the decisive voter might even be a pair of an old and young individual revealing identical tax preferences.

In order to regard the main arguments of bequest taxation – namely, the taxation of unearned wealth in contrast to earned labor income, as well as redistribution between the rich minority and the poor majority, I distinguish two different scenarios in the following. In the first case the focus lies on the composition of taxes on labor income of the young and on bequests received by the old. Holding constant budget requirements of the government, individual preferences on both tax alternatives are observed. In contrast, introducing government transfers to the old in form of public pensions, I concentrate on redistributive aspects in the second case. Funded by tax revenues, the amount of pension payments is endogenously determined by the tax rate on bequests, holding fixed labor income taxes. Hence, whereas I observe solely intergenerational tax effects in case 1, the introduction of public pensions additionally includes intra- and intergenerational redistribution in case 2.

4.2.2.1 Case 1: Voting on labor income and bequest tax rates

The government is assumed to face an exogenous budget $\overline{g}$ in both periods. In t this can be funded by a combination of taxes levied on young individuals' gross income and on old individuals' inheritances. However, given there are only old individuals in the second period the revenue requirements have to be covered solely by bequest taxes in $t+1$.

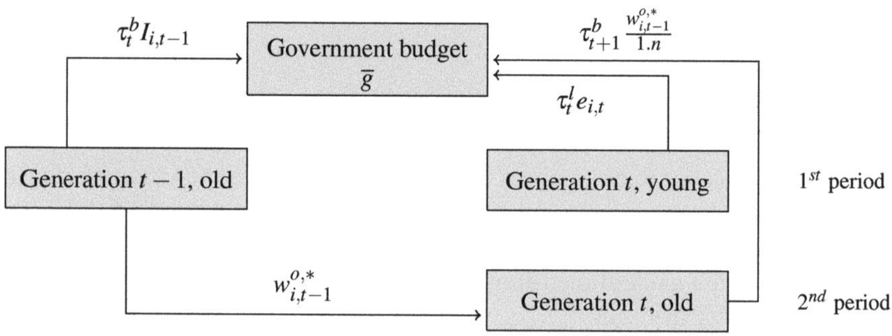

Hence, the government budget constraint for both periods reveals, respectively

$$\tau_t^l(1+n)e_t + \tau_t^b I_{t-1} = \tau_{t+1}^b \frac{w_{t-1}^o}{1+n} = \overline{g}. \tag{4.11}$$

In order to determine the optimal tax policy, the government holds a referendum on the estate tax rate. The one preferred by the median-voter will be chosen, and the tax on labor earnings is then set as a residual to finance the exogenous budget requirements. Thus, the effect of inheritance taxation on the labor income tax can be calculated by $\frac{\partial \tau_t^l}{\partial \tau_t^b} = -\frac{I_{t-1}}{e_t l_t (1+n)}$. Potential tax reduction on labor earnings, associated with a bequest tax increase, depend on the ratio of parent's average inheritance to child's average labor income. The larger the inheritance tax base compared to the labor income tax base the higher are tax reductions associated with an estate tax increase. Likewise, the larger average labor income and the higher population growth the less perceptible are labor income tax allowances. The tax effect on future bequest taxation, however, is determined by public revenue requirements and parent's average bequests, which vary with τ_t^b itself. Thus, it holds $\frac{\partial \tau_{t+1}^b}{\partial \tau_t^b} = \frac{\left(\partial \frac{\overline{g}}{w_{t-1}^o/(1+n)}\right)}{\partial \tau_t^b}$. Old and young individual's economic decisions, illustrated in (4.9) and (4.10), hence depend solely on the median voter's decision on τ_t^b.

Voter's preferences. For the old generation, a tax on estates in t directly reduces taxable initial wealth by $\tau_t^b I_{i,t-1}$. Savings and therewith wealth transfers decrease, which at the same time increases future inheritance tax rates, in order to ensure the government budget. Capitalistic utility gained by the amount of present and future net wealth thus is diminished twofold – by lower savings today and higher tax rates in the future. Hence, the individual-specific welfare effect of inheritance taxation on the old generation's indirect utility can be implicitly defined using (4.9) and (4.6)

$$\frac{\partial v_{i,t-1}(\tau_t^b)}{\partial \tau_t^b} = \begin{cases} u'(\cdot)\left(-I_{i,t-1} - \frac{\partial w_{i,t-1}^{o,*}}{\partial \tau_t^b}\right) + \gamma \frac{\partial w_{i,t-1}^{o,*}}{\partial \tau_t^b}\left(1 + \frac{1 - \frac{\partial \tau_{t+1}^b}{\partial \tau_t^b}}{1+\sigma}\right) - \frac{\gamma w_{i,t-1}^{o,*}\frac{\partial \tau_{t+1}^b}{\partial \tau_t^b}}{1+\sigma} \\ \qquad \text{if } 1 + I_{i,t-1}(1-\tau_t^b) > c_{i,t-1}^{o,*}, \\ 0 \qquad \text{otherwise.} \end{cases}$$

It is straightforward to show that under positive taxable wealth $I_{i,t-1} > 0$ and positive bequests $w_{i,t-1}^{o,*} > 0$ the derivative is always negative for those parents leaving positive bequests. Taxation of wealth transfers therefore always leads to decreasing welfare for most of the old individuals. Solely those who neither receive taxable initial wealth nor save and bequeath themselves remain undistorted.

The young generation, however, faces two opposing effects when an inheritance tax is levied in t. Since labor income tax is set as a residual to finance public revenues, increasing bequest tax rates, on the one hand, reduce children's labor income liabilities, resulting in larger net labor earnings and hence increase present consumption and savings. On the other hand, expected inheritances in $t+1$ decline and at the same time are levied with a higher bequest tax. The welfare effect on a young individual, can thus be determined by the derivative of the children's indirect utility function (4.10)

$$\frac{\partial v_{i,t}(\tau_t^b)}{\partial \tau_t^b} = \frac{\frac{\partial c_{i,t-1}^{o,*}}{\partial \tau_t^b}}{1+\sigma} + u'(\cdot)\left(\frac{\partial c_{i,t-1}^{o,*}}{\partial \tau_t^b} - e_{i,t}\frac{\partial \tau_t^l}{\partial \tau_t^b}\right) + \frac{(1-\tau_{t+1}^b)\frac{\partial w_{i,t-1}^{o,*}}{\partial \tau_t^b}}{1+n} - \frac{w_{i,t-1}^{o,*}\frac{\partial \tau_{t+1}^b}{\partial \tau_t^b}}{1+n}. \tag{4.12}$$

Apparently, direct utility changes in the first period are positive, given that labor income taxes decline with rising estate tax rates. However, due to diminished parental savings and hence lower bequests, present tax policy also impacts second period taxation by reducing the future tax base. Lower expected inheritances and higher expected tax rates reduce children's discounted second period utility and thus induce negative effects even in the present. Whether the sign of the young individual's welfare effect is positive or negative depends on the individual ratio of expected inheritances and own labor income as well as on the required tax rates in both periods.

When it comes to vote on the tax rate, each individual optimizes her tax liabilities. Accordingly, she votes for that tax rate maximizing her lifetime utility, already anticipating the aftermath of her present decisions on future tax policy. In order to determine the decisive voter in a society being heterogeneous according to wealth (determined by initial endowments and initial abilities) and age, the tax impacts on parents and children have to be combined. Then, by sorting individual tax preferences one is able to identify the majoritarian tax policy.

The median-voter. Given there is no family link between generations and parents neither receive labor income nor compensatory public transfer, the entire old generation will either favor a zero inheritance tax and thereby high labor income taxes (if $I_{i,t-1} > 0$) or is indifferent to both alternatives (if $I_{i,t-1} = 0$ and $w^o_{i,t-1} = 0$). In the latter case I assume these individuals to abstain from voting.[72] Even though the majority of the old generation militates against a tax on wealth transfers, they nevertheless cannot command society's majority, due to positive population growth and voting abstention. The children's preferences can therefore be revealed as the decisive factor in this voting process.

For the children to favor an estate tax, the utility gain by labor income tax allowances must exceed the utility loss due to expected inheritance reductions and future tax liabilities. These utility changes consist of pure income effects on labor earnings and future inheritances (E^l_i and E^b_i) as well as substitutive effects produced by shifting income and wealth over time and hence changing the individuals' optimal consumption paths.[73] However, whereas the old generation's preference distribution is shaped according to the right-skewed inheritance distribution $H(\cdot)$, the shape of the children's preference distribution is undetermined. It depends on the labor income distribution $G(\cdot)$ and the wealth distribution of their parents $H(\cdot)$. Thus, the young individuals' preference distribution depends on the correlation of own initial abilities, which determine labor income, and parent's inheritances. Therein, two extremes can be distinguished:

- If own income opportunities and parental wealth are *perfectly positively correlated*, young individuals with high labor income opportunities concur-

[72] Voting is assumed to incur voting costs ε – e.g. opportunity costs – which are supposed to be infinitesimal small. However, individuals whose benefits from tax policy are always zero and who are thus indifferent to inheritance or labor income taxation will abstain from voting. Their benefits from voting are always negative, even if voting is an extremely low cost activity.

[73] The pure income effects can be calculated by $E^l_i : \left(\frac{\partial \tau^l_t}{\partial \tau^b_t}\, \tau^b_t + \tau^l_t\right) e_{i,t}$ for labor income and by E^b_i : $\frac{\left[\left(\frac{\partial \tau^{b,*}_{t+1}}{\partial w^o_{t-1}} \frac{\partial w^{o,*}_{t-1}}{\partial \tau^b_t}\, \tau^b_t\right) + \tau^{b,*}_{t+1}\right]\left[\frac{\partial w^{o,*}_{i,t-1}}{\partial \tau^b_t}\, \tau^b_t + w^{o,*}_{i,t-1}\right]}{(1+\sigma)(1+n)}$ for future inheritances.

rently face high inheritances and reverse. Even though the ratio of labor income and expected inheritances is the same for all individuals, the income effects on future inheritances are not. Given the tax effect on parental inheritances is increasing in wealth, the income effect on future inheritances is larger the richer the children. The effect on labor earnings, however, is proportional and thus becomes less significant with increasing inheritance expectations. Hence, I find a right-skewed preference distribution in accordance with the parent's inheritance distribution that is shifted to the left, due to the positive effects on labor earnings. The decisive voter would then be a wealthy child with high innate ability.

- However, if income opportunities and parental wealth are *perfectly negatively correlated*, all individuals with low initial income face high inheritances and reverse. Under these circumstances, the negative income effect on future inheritances is smaller the richer the children. By similar argumentation, I hence observe a left-skewed distribution of children's preferences. The median voter of society is then located among these children with low earning possibilities and high expected inheritances.

Even though, theoretically, any shape of distribution is likely to emerge, empirical evidence leads to the assumption that parental wealth and children's income are positively (nevertheless, not perfectly) correlated.[74] However, since parental wealth is more unequally distributed than children's income, a majority of the young generation will inherit less than their labor income and only a few children will inherit more than they earn by own labor. Thus I can suppose the preference distribution, denominated as $F(\cdot)$, to be right-skewed with bounded support $[\underline{E^b+E^l}, \overline{E^b+E^l}]$ on the interval $[-1,1]$. A hypothetical distribution is illustrated in Figure 4.4. For all individuals located on the positive axis, negative wealth effects associated with a tax on bequests preponderate. Those located on the negative axis, however, face larger labor income tax allowances than expected inheritance losses – they favor a tax on bequests.
Society's median voter can thus be identified by the following cumulative distribution

$$H(I_{M,t-1}) + (1+n)F((E^b+E^l)_M) = [1-H(I_{M,t-1})] + (1+n)[1-F((E^b+E^l)_M)], \quad (4.13)$$

[74]Empirical findings show that individuals with higher income also own more wealth, and that substantial part of this wealth is regarded to inheritances. See e.g. Gale and Scholz (1994) and Modigliani (1988).

Figure 4.4: Case 1: Exemplary preference distribution of old and young voters

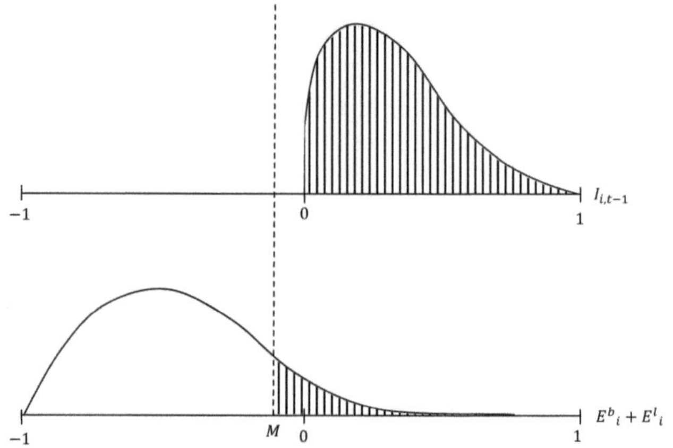

which can be simplified to

$$H(I_{M,t-1}) + (1+n)F((E^b + E^l)_M) = 1 + \frac{n}{2}. \tag{4.14}$$

The left-hand side of equation (4.13) represents all parents and children who prefer an estate tax rate higher or equal to that preferred by the society's median voter. The reverse is true for the right-hand side. To identify the median voter parent and child the number of voters on both sides of the median must be equalized. Since E_i^l is negative the children's distribution is shifted to the left, implying that each child votes like a poorer parent. The society's median voter is located left of the old median voter and right of the young median voter. The coalition right of society's median voter thus consists of a majority of parents and a minority of children. Accordingly the coalition on the left is composed by reversed majorities. To further analyze how the median voter's tax preferences are determined in equilibrium, I use the following example.

Example 4.1. Let the old and young individual's present consumption be logarithmic, $\ln(c^o_{i,t-1})$ and $\ln(c^y_{i,t})$. Society's average labor income is further given by $e_t = 0.45$ and parental average inheritance is set at $I_{t-1} = 0.3$. The government is supposed to have identical average budget requirements in both periods, which are exogenously given by $\overline{g} = 0.3$. Society's growth rate is assumed to be $n = 0.1$, time preference rate $\sigma = 0.1$, and the intensity of the parents' capitalist spirit $\gamma = 2$. The optimal wealth transfer of the average parent w^o_{t-1} at $\tau^b_t = 0$ can be calculated by

$$w^{o,*}_{t-1} = 1 + I_{i,t-1}(1-\tau^b_t) - \frac{1}{\gamma(1+\frac{1-\tau^b_{t+1}}{1+\sigma})} = 0.994,$$

where the expected future inheritance tax rate reveals $\tau^b_{t+1} = \frac{\bar{g}}{w^{o,*}_{t-1}} = 0.33$.

As, in the present case society's median voter is among the young individuals, I can calculate the preferred tax rate on parental inheritances by maximizing children's indirect utility with changing τ^b_t.

$$\max_{\tau^b_t} \quad e_{i,t}(1-\tau^l_t) - \left(\frac{1}{\gamma(1+\frac{1-\tau^t_{t+1}}{1+\sigma})(1+n)}\right)(1-\tau^b_{t+1}) - \frac{1}{\frac{1}{1+\sigma}} \quad (4.15)$$

Table 4.1 illustrates young voter's estate tax preferences which are shaped by individual taxable labor earnings and own parent's taxable inheritance.

Table 4.1: Case 1: Young voter's preferences on τ^b_t.

		$I_{t-1,i}$							
		0	0.1	0.2	0.3	0.5	0.6	0.7
	0	indiff.	0	0	0	0	0	0
	0.1	1	0	0	0	0	0	0
	0.2	1	0.052	0	0	0	0	0
	0.3	1	0.433	0	0	0	0	0
$e_{t,i}$	0.5	1	0.910	0.314	0.014	0	0	0
	0.6	1	1	0.469	0.167	0	0	0
	0.8	1	1	0.699	0.408	0.043	0	0
	0.9	1	1	0.786	0.498	0.153	0.011	0
	1	1	1	0.861	0.575	0.245	0.115	0.020

Thus, it can be observed that the composition of children's wealth determines whether a young individual favors high or low inheritance taxes in t.

The higher own labor income compared to expected inheritances, the higher the preferences for wealth transfer taxes and reverse.

Case 1 shows that the majority of a population, which is shaped by capitalistic preferences, prefers labor income to bequest taxes. This is due to the fact that the latter affects the old generation twice in lifetime. First by reduced inheritances and again by reduced transfers to future generations by which their capitalistic utility is diminished. Similarly, with present inheritance taxation, the young individuals being life-cycle savers only, face smaller gross bequests and at the same time higher future bequest tax rate. Such that children's net bequests are reduced twofold. Thereby, the tax effect on wealth transfers is stronger than on labor income. Children expecting large bequests (in Example 1 this holds for $I_{t-1,i} \geq 0.7$), will repudiate inheritance taxation irrespective of their own labor earnings.

4.2.2.2 Case 2: Voting on redistributive bequest taxes

I modify the previous setting by endogenizing government revenues g. I assume that these are transferred to the old generation by public pensions f under a balanced budget. In doing so, public transfers consist of the same non-negative lump-sum payment for every old individual. Given taxes on labor income of the young and on inheritances of the old are collected to finance these public payments, such a pension system redistributes across and within the generations.

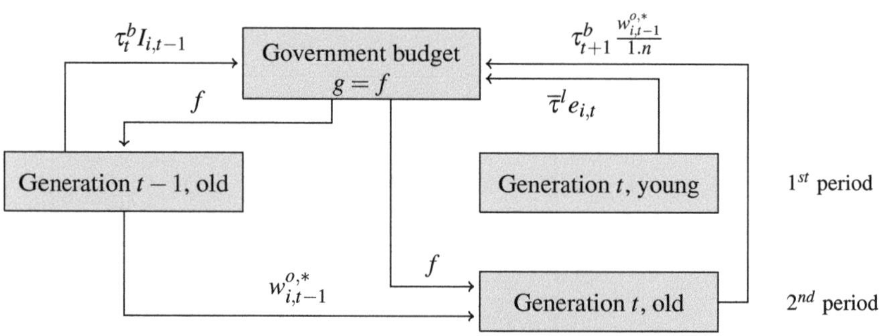

I assume further complete commitment to the pension system over time. In period t individuals are to vote on the tax rate τ_t^b and thereby on f, determining a policy that remains forever. Hence, current votes of the political agents determine present and future policy. To guarantee a one-dimensional policy space I set proportional labor income taxes $\overline{\tau}^l$ as fixed, such that a minimum of government revenues and hence public pensions is given by $g^{min} = \overline{\tau}^l (1+n)\, e_t$. Additional revenues and thereby higher public transfers can be achieved by supplemental taxation of bequests in the first period. In the second period, the revenue requirements have to be funded by bequest taxes only. Hence, the government budget constraint reveals for both periods

$$\overline{\tau}^l(1+n)e_t + \tau_t^b I_{t-1} = \tau_{t+1}^b \frac{w_{t-1}^o}{1+n} = g = f \tag{4.16}$$

To approve the optimal amount of public pension, the government holds a referendum in t determining the optimal estate tax rate in the present period.

The economic equilibrium shown in Section 4.2.1 has to be slightly modified in accordance to the new underlying assumptions, given that both generations receive additional pension payments when old. (4.3) and (4.5) change to

$$c_{i,t-1}^o = 1 + I_{i,t-1}(1-\tau_t^b) + f - w_{i,t-1}^o, \tag{4.3'}$$

$$c_{i,t}^o = w_{i,t}^y + \frac{w_{i,t-1}^o}{1+n}(1-\tau_{t+1}^b) + f. \tag{4.5'}$$

Maximizing (4.1) and (4.2) under these budget constraints reveals optimal economic decisions of both generations still to depend on present and future tax rates, but additionally also on potential public pension payments. The modified indirect utility for old and young then holds, respectively

$$v_{i,t-1}^o(\tau_t^b) = u(1 + I_{i,t-1}(1-\tau_t^b) - w_{i,t-1}^{o,*} + f) + w_{i,t-1}^{o,*}\gamma\left(1 + \frac{1-\tau_{t+1}^b}{1+\sigma}\right), \tag{4.9'}$$

$$v_{i,t}^y(\tau_t^b) = u(1 + e_{i,t}(1 - \overline{\tau}^l) - c_{i,t}^{o,*} + \frac{w_{i,t-1}^{o,*}}{1+n}(1 - \tau_{t+1}^b) + f) + \frac{c_{i,t}^{o,*}}{1+\sigma}. \tag{4.10'}$$

Voter's preferences. Contrasting to Case 1, now the old generation is not entirely worse off as soon as inheritances are taxed. This is due to the fact that public revenues are redistributed among the old. Thus, even though a bequest tax directly reduces taxable initial wealth resources by $\tau_t^b(I_{i,t-1})$ in t, additional pension payments of $\tau_t^b I_{t-1}$ are transferred to the old and may counterbalance their individual tax duty. Such that those benefiting more by pension payments than they lose by additional tax liabilities, will favor higher public transfers and hence the additional taxation of estates. On the other hand, all other old individuals, whose present and future tax liabilities outweigh public pension receipts, will repudiate supplemental taxation. One might suppose that those parents with own inheritances smaller (larger) than the average initial wealth transfer will favor (repudiate) additional taxation. However, due to perfect policy commitment, voting for higher public pensions today also leads to higher public transfers in the future. This might reduce parent's capitalistic utility, given their own bequests consequently are to be higher taxed in the future. Hence, by use of (4.9'), (4.3'), and (4.16), the individual-specific welfare effect of inheritance taxation on the old generation can be written as

$$\frac{\partial v^o_{i,t-1}(\tau^b_t)}{\partial \tau^b_t} = \left(I_{t-1} - I_{i,t-1} - \frac{\partial w^{o,*}_{i,t-1}}{\partial \tau^b_t} \right) \frac{\partial u(\cdot)}{\partial \tau^b_t} - \gamma (1 + \frac{1-\tau^b_{t+1}}{1+\sigma}) \frac{\partial w^{o,*}_{i,t-1}}{\partial \tau^b_t}. \quad (4.17)$$

Whether the sign of parent's utility is positive or negative essentially depends on the difference between average and individual inheritances as well as on the tax induced changes of optimal wealth holdings $w^{o,*}_{i,t-1}$.

The young generation does not face any effect on their present labor income when an additional tax is levied in t. Since labor income is taxed at a fixed rate, current period budget remains undistorted. However, present taxation of estates directly affects children's inheritances, their corresponding future tax liabilities as well as own pensions receipts in $t+1$. Thus, it can be supposed that all children whose parents receive initial wealth transfers lower than the additional pension payments favor a tax on bequests. Thereby they can increase their own future inheritances as well as their own pension payments, taking into account that higher public transfers inevitably induce higher bequest taxes on their own inheritances. All other young individuals whose parents inherit initial endowments larger than potential pension receipts will object to an additional bequest tax. They can expect larger wealth transfers by their parents than via public pensions. Thus, by use of (4.10'), (4.4), (4.5') , and (4.16) the welfare effect on a young individual due to additional bequest taxation in t can be determined by

$$\frac{\partial v^y_{i,t}(\tau^b_t)}{\partial \tau^b_t} =$$

$$\left(I_{t-1} - \frac{\partial c^{o,*}_{i,t}}{\partial \tau^b_t} - \frac{w^{o,*}_{i,t-1}}{1+n} \frac{\partial \tau^b_{t+1}}{\partial \tau^b_t} + (1-\tau^b_{t+1}) \frac{\partial \frac{w^o_{i,t-1}}{1+n}}{\partial \tau^b_t} \right) \frac{\partial u(\cdot)}{\partial \tau^b_t} + \frac{\frac{\partial c^{o,*}_{i,t}}{\partial \tau^b_t}}{1+\sigma}. \quad (4.18)$$

Whether young individual's welfare effect is positive or negative is independent of children's own labor income. Responsible for the tax effects on children's welfare are solely parent's inheritances and consequently the associated changes in bequests and thereby in future tax rates.[75] Thus, parental wealth determines children's optimal consumption over time and dictates whether to prefer higher bequests or additional pension payments in the future.

Therefore, when a referendum on the inheritance tax rate or equivalently on the amount of public pensions is held, each voter will optimize her lifetime utility. To be able to find the decisive voter in this heterogeneous society tax preferences have to be distinguished by age and wealth. Thereby, a tax policy favored by a majority of voters can be determined.

The median-voter. Since public transfers redistribute within and across generations, proponents as well as opponents of inheritance taxation can be found among both generations. Thus, unlike case 1, to characterize the society's median voter, young and old political agents have to be combined. The median voter will then be determined by a pair of a parent and a child (not necessarily his own), which exhibit the same tax preferences.

The old generation's preferences are shaped by their individual specific initial wealth, which is distributed according to $H(\cdot)$. However, since all of them receive a public pension, the distribution is shifted to the left by f. The higher the inheritance, the less perceptible are these pension payments and the less favored are inheritance taxes.

Similarly, young voter's tax preferences are also determined by their own parent's inheritances. Since the wealth receipts of the old generation define the amount of bequests given to the descendants, children will favor inheritance taxation as long as their expected net inheritance decrease (E_i^b) is smaller than the discounted public transfer f. This holds for all those children whose parents receive small inheritances and hence bequeath little.[76] The inheritance tax effect on the young generation E_i^b is shaped according to a endogenous distribution $S(\cdot)$ determined by parents' saving behavior and the present tax rates.

Even though $S(\cdot)$ is indirectly defined by parental wealth, it has a different shape compared to the parent's distribution. This is, on the one hand, due to the fact that the fraction of parental wealth transferred to the children rises overproportionally with the initial wealth level.[77] On the other hand, taxation of inheritances affects

[75] The tax effect on future estate taxes is determined by public revenue requirements and parent's average bequest, which, other than in case 1, both vary with τ_t^b. Thus, it holds $\frac{\partial \tau_{t+1}^b}{\partial \tau_t^b} = \frac{\partial \frac{g}{w_{t-1}^o}}{\partial \tau_t^b}$.

[76] Like in case 1 $E_i^b = \frac{\left[\left(\frac{\partial \tau_{t+1}^{b,*}}{\partial w_{t-1}^o} \frac{\partial w_{t-1}^{o,*}}{\partial \tau_t^b} \tau_t^b\right) + \tau_{t+1}^{b,*}\right]\left[\frac{\partial w_{i,t-1}^{o,*}}{\partial \tau_t^b} \tau_t^b + w_{i,t-1}^{o,*}\right]}{(1+\sigma)(1+n)}$.

[77] The intensity by which bequests rise with increasing initial wealth depends on the functional form of utility gained by consumption.

children's welfare in different ways and intensities across the wealth levels.[78] Intuitively, the wealthy suffer whilst the poor benefit. A hypothetical preference distribution of both generations is depicted in Figure 4.5.

Figure 4.5: Case 2: Exemplary preference distribution of old and young voters

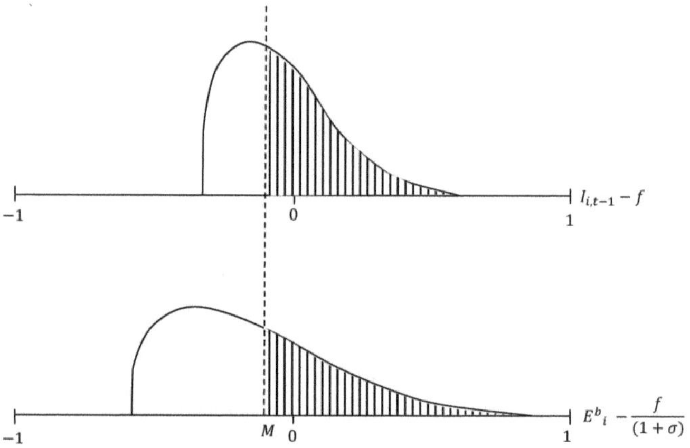

For all individuals on the positive axis, negative wealth effects associated with a tax on bequests preponderate. Those on the negative axis, however, face larger pension payments than tax liabilities. Thus they favor a tax on bequests.
The median-voter can then be identified according to

$$H((I_{M,t-1}-f))+(1+n)\,S((E_M^b-\frac{f}{1+\sigma}))$$
$$=[1-G((I_{M,t-1}-f))]+(1+n)[1-F((E_M^b-\frac{f}{1+\sigma}))], \quad (4.19)$$

which can be simplified to

$$H((I_{M,t-1}-f))+(1+n)\,S((E_M^b-\frac{f}{1+\sigma}))=1+\frac{n}{2}. \quad (4.20)$$

[78]Future bequests increase for children having poor parents, whereas they are reduced for those of rich parents. Additionally, second period tax rate increases, affecting all individuals proportionally. However, public pension payments can compensate the tax duty for the low wealth individuals, whereas those receiving large inheritances are worse off.

The left-hand (right-hand) side of equation (4.19) represents all parents and children who prefer an estate tax rate higher (lower) or equal to that preferred by society's median voter. To identify the median voter pair consisting of a parent and child, the number of voters on both sides of the median must be equalized. Since public pension is given as a lump-sum payment to every old individual in both generations it compensates the tax duty of each individual. Hence, the distribution of parents as well as children is shifted to the left. In order to receive more detailed information on the tax preferences of society's median-voter pair, I use the following example.

Example 4.2. Let, analog to Example 4.1, parents' and children's present consumption be logarithmic, $\ln(c^o_{i,t-1})$ and $\ln(c^y_{i,t})$. Society's average labor income is further given by $e_t = 0.45$ and parental average inheritance is set at $I_{t-1} = 0.3$. The government is supposed to finance its minimum budget requirements by labor income taxation levied on the current young. The tax rate is assumed to be $\overline{\tau}^l = 0.2$. Additional revenues can be generated by inheritance taxation such that $g_t = 0.2e_t + \tau^b_t I_{t-1} = f$. Since I assume complete commitment to the pension system, public revenues are to be the same in both periods, $g_t = g_{t+1}$. Thus the tax rate levied on inheritances in the future period is explicitly defined by current political decisions. Society's growth rate is again assumed to be $n = 0.1$, the time preference rate $\sigma = 0.1$ and the intensity of the parental capitalist spirit $\gamma = 2$.

Contrasting to Case 1, parents receive a public pension in addition to their inheritance. Hence, those parents with taxable inheritances smaller than potential additional pension payments are supposed to opt for a tax on estates. Given that for the present example, the optimal wealth transfer of the average parent w^o_{t-1} under $\tau^b_t = 0$ is calculated by

$$w^{o,*}_{t-1} = 1 + I_{i,t-1}(1-\tau^b_t) + (\overline{\tau}^l e_t + \tau^b_t I_{t-1}) - \frac{1}{\gamma(1+\frac{1-\tau^b_{t+1}}{1+\sigma})} = 1.12,$$

and the expected future inheritance tax rate reveals $\tau^b_{t+1} = \frac{g_t}{w^{o,*}_{t-1}} = 0.10$. Table 4.2 and Figure 4.6 then illustrates parent's preferences on inheritance tax rates and thereby on corresponding public pension payments, according to the level of their initial inheritances.

It can be observed that with public pension payments, poorer parents will support an additional inheritance tax. By intra-generational redistribution they enhance own welfare, even if being taxed themselves. However, future inheritance taxation inevitably increases with present bequest taxes. There-

Table 4.2: Case 2: Old voter's preferences on τ_t^b and f.

$I_{t-1,i}$	0	0.1	0.15	0.2	0.25	0.3	≥0.35
τ_t^b	1	0.885	0.671	0.452	0.237	0.035	0
f	0.39	0.366	0.301	0.236	0.171	0.111	0.1
$\tau_t^b I_{t-1,i}$	0	0.086	0.101	0.090	0.059	0.011	0
$f-\tau_t^b I_{t-1,i}$	0.39	0.28	0.2	0.146	0.112	0.1	0.1

fore, the benefit gained by higher public pensions decreases with own taxable wealth and diminishes parent's utility gained by capitalistic bequest. Hence, it can be shown that the closer the value of taxable inherited wealth to the value of potential pension payments the lower the preferences for additional taxation.

Other than in Case 1, the young individuals' tax preferences are shaped by their parent's inheritance only, independent of their own labor earnings. Hence, by maximizing children's indirect utility with changing τ_t^b, Table 4.3 and Figure 4.7 reveals the preferred tax rates under redistributive policy.

Table 4.3: Case 2: Young voter's preferences on τ_t^b and f.

$I_{t-1,i}$	0	0.1	0.28	0.285	0.288	0.3	1
τ_t^b	1	1	0.964	0.321	0.087	0	0
f	0.39	0.39	0.389	0.196	0.186	0.1	0.1
$\frac{w_{i,t-1}^o}{1+n}$	0.746	0.839	1.005	1.010	1.013	1.024	1.663
τ_{t+1}^b	0.390	0.390	0.379	0.191	0.122	0.097	0.097
$\tau_{t+1}^b \frac{w_{i,t-1}^o}{1+n}$	0.291	0.327	0.381	0.192	0.123	0.099	0.161
$f-\tau_{t+1}^b \frac{w_{i,t-1}^o}{1+n}$	0.099	0.063	0.008	0.004	0.003	0.001	-0.061

It can be shown that children's preferences are much more polarized, due to the fact that the taxation of inheritances benefits poor and harms rich children twofold. Whereas the former face increasing parental bequests and high public pensions compared to family transfers, the latter inherit

Figure 4.6: Case 2: Old voter's preferences on τ_t^b according to initial inheritance

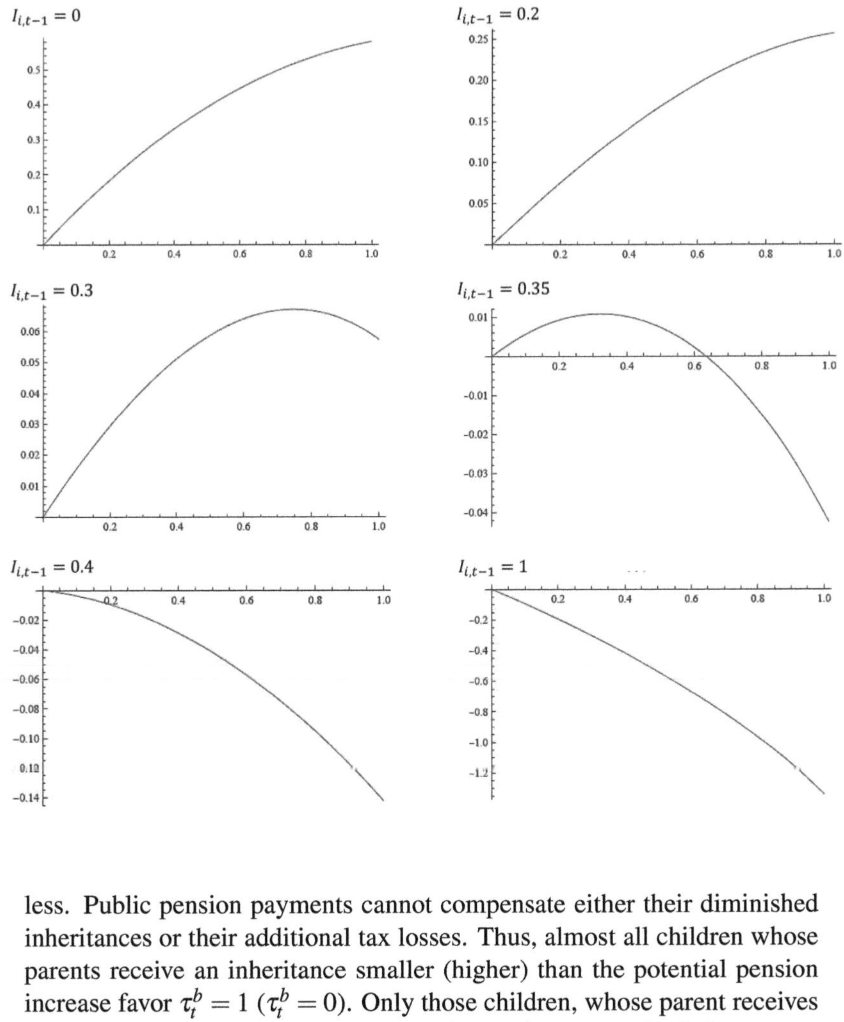

less. Public pension payments cannot compensate either their diminished inheritances or their additional tax losses. Thus, almost all children whose parents receive an inheritance smaller (higher) than the potential pension increase favor $\tau_t^b = 1$ ($\tau_t^b = 0$). Only those children, whose parent receives inheritances smaller but very close to the maximum pension's increment, reveal tax preferences lying between these two extremes.

This example illustrates that the introduction of public transfers divides society's tax preferences according to wealth levels. By holding constant labor income

Figure 4.7: Case 2: Young voter's preferences on τ_t^b according to parent's initial inheritance

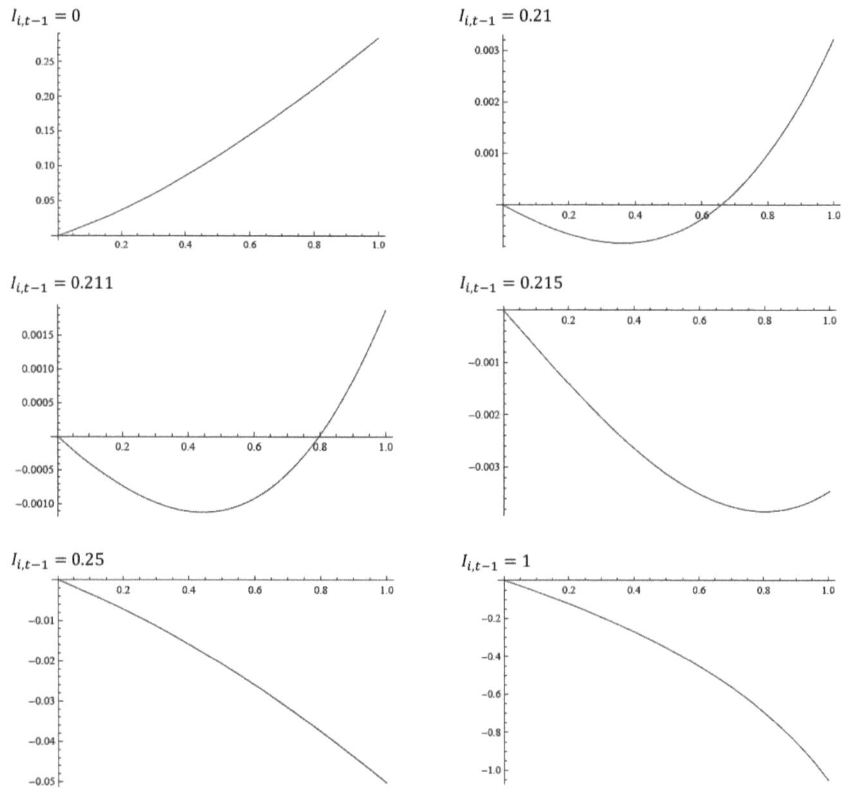

taxes, individuals form coalitions according to wealth, almost irrespective of age. Case 2 thus reveals that a capitalistic society favors positive bequest taxes as soon as they redistribute across and within generations. The more unequal the distribution of wealth, the higher the preferred tax rate on capitalistic bequests. Generally, it can be observed that poorer (and to some extent older) voters prefer higher public pensions, as they benefit more from either intra- or intergenerational redistribution.

In summary, the politically viable bequest tax rate crucially depends on the decisive voter's wealth, affected by an inheritance tax. So that its determination relies on the wealth distribution in society, which on grounds of empirical evidence, can be supposed to be right-skewed.

If tax revenues are not redistributed in society, voters solely optimize their personal tax liabilities. For the taxation of estates, voter's tax preferences can then be explicitly divided by age, with the old opposing inheritance taxation completely and the median voter to be found among the young individuals. As all individuals are further heterogeneous according to wealth, the politically viable tax rate is likely to be low, given that a young, wealthy voter decides upon the tax rate.

However, as soon as revenues are used for redistribution across and within generations, the decisive voter prefers considerably higher taxes. This is due to the fact that redistribution benefits the young as well as the old voters similarly. Given that the median voter is poorer than the average, she is less affected by taxation but more favored by public transfers. As a result, this leads to higher taxes than economically optimal.

Generally, it can be observed that the aforementioned effects, which have been analyzed separately, are much rather combined in practice. Both results lead to the conclusion that the richer and older individuals become, the lower the individual preferences to levy a wealth transfer tax.

4.3 Extensions

In the following I study the effects on the political equilibrium tax rate when the underlying parameters change. Therefore I analyze how the economic power of wealthy individuals can be translated into political influence. Further, I focus on changes in population growth rate n, in order to identify the effects of an aging population on wealth transfer taxes. Finally, I consider how imperfect policy commitment changes the political equilibrium.

4.3.1 The economic power of the very rich

Analyzing the existence of dynamic effects of expropriating the rich corresponds to the common belief that economic power is often directly translated into political power. Similar to Breyer and Ursprung (1998) it can be assumed that those affected by an estate tax will adapt their economic decisions or even try to evade taxation completely, when being taxed too heavily. Various conceivable possibilities exist, reaching from moving to other jurisdictions to using direct political influence, e.g.

by the formation of pressure groups. However, all these avoidance methods can be considered as a threat to force the government to do what is in favor of the affected.

Following Becker (1985) governmental tax and redistribution decisions are thus not only determined by the median voter. They might rather be oriented towards those being able to exert the strongest pressure on the government. This idea can be applied to the present model by giving different weights to each voter.[79]

Hence, suppose a parameter $0 < z_{t,i} \leq 1$ that describes the possibilities to exert political influence. I assume that this parameter crucially depends on the capital held by an individual, the publicity she enjoys and the trustworthiness of her tax avoidance options. All these attributes are most applicable on wealthy individuals being able to exploit their influence, for example by threatening the government to reduce the number of jobs by shifting them abroad or to cut financial support.

In order to identify the decisive voter, the government has to regard this wealth-dependent scope of political influence. Compared to Section 4.2, the median voter can then be identified by weighting individuals stronger the more wealth they hold. Leading to the result that although the very wealthy are defeated in numbers they are able to use their economic power to gain political influence. The cumulative distribution of parents and children in Figure 4.4 and 4.5 thereby becomes flatter with a thicker right tail, reflecting the emphasis given to the wealthy. Thereby, society's median shifts to the right. An increasing influence of economic power on the political decision process hence induces the individuals, being most affected by the estate tax, to prevail. They can bias the estate tax rate subject to their own interests, such that τ_t^b will decrease.

Applied to current developments, this observation suggests that the increasing tax competition among countries, due to heterogeneous tax policies, strengthens the influence and interests of the rich. Since their wealth is most affected by bequest taxation and at the same time consists of (highly) mobile capital assets, they are able to exert enhanced political pressure to pursue their personal tax preferences. It can be assumed that the wealthy will take advantage of their economic power even more in the future.

4.3.2 Aging societies

Changes in population's age composition are a common challenge for most modern societies. Since the baby-boom decades in the 50s and 60s, many societies in Europe face declining fertility rates. Projected onto the future, this tendency will

[79] Similarly Coughlin, Mueller and Murrell (1990) integrate the influence of pressure groups into a two-party model, by additionally weighting the utility gained by the number of votes with a parameter describing the political influence.

cause fundamental changes in society's age structure, and will lead to substantial modification of the political weights of different age cohorts. Thus, population's aging might explain the observed variations in the tax mix of many western societies.

Theories on demographic change with regard to political equilibria can be based on conside-rations of Razin and Sadka (2007). They explore the relationship of an aging population and the size of the welfare state, showing that the welfare system does not necessarily expand when society ages. Similarly, Mateos-Planas (2010) scrutinizes the effects of an aging society on labor and capital tax rates. Revealing that, against expectations, aging populations might even favor increasing capital taxation.

Applied to the present setting, I assume the population growth rate n to become negative and thus the average age in society to rise. Consequently, I face changing political majorities and therewith a new decisive voter. Compared to the political equilibria evolved in Section 4.2, the shrinkage of the young generation bestows more political weight to the old generation. A negative population growth rate, moreover, implies the existence of fewer descendants and thus induces the amount of per capita wealth receipt of each child to increase. However, at the same time the work force in society declines, which reduces government's revenue opportunities.

Hence, on the one hand, the larger the decline in population, the larger is each young indivi-dual's share of inherited to total lifetime wealth. Thereby, children's preferences for the taxation of bequests decrease. On the other hand, if the number of children is reduced, taxes on labor income rise, in order to finance average public revenues. Thus, labor income taxation as an alternative to inheritance taxation becomes less attractive. To simplify the analysis, I assume that these two ambiguous effects compensate each other, abstracting from the individual tax effects on the voter's behavior. Rather, I concentrate on the effects on political majorities.

Under the absence of redistributive public transfers (Case 1), negative population growth induces lower inheritance taxes. The old generation, favoring labor income taxes, gains more political weight such that, compared to Figure 4.4, the median voter is shifted to the right. Thus, the political equilibrium is determined by an even wealthier child or perhaps even by an old individual. Whereas the former might still favor a low inheritance tax, the latter will rather call for an abolition of bequest taxation. However, as soon as revenues are redistributed within society (Case 2), the net effect is ambiguous: a lower population growth, can then lead to either higher or lower estate tax rates and thereby to more or less inter- and intragenerational redistribution, depending on the specific properties of the children's utility function and of the initial wealth distribution.

It is obvious that current demographic developments do not only have economic and social impacts, but rather will entirely change political majorities. Leading to higher or lower wealth transfer taxation, however, crucially depends on the income and wealth distribution in society. Nonetheless, a slight tendency to lower wealth taxes might be observable, given that older individuals in general are more aware of their own intergenerational wealth transfer and therewith favor alternative taxes by which they themselves are not affected any more.

4.3.3 Policy commitment

The results of Section 4.2 crucially depend on the assumption that voters decide on the inheritance tax rate under complete policy commitment, anticipating that the present decision holds forever. Given that this assumption is really restrictive, it is interesting to consider the effects exerted by changing the length of policy commitment. It can be shown that the shorter the election periods the more biased the policy outcome to the median voter's short-term preferences.

Hence, by extending the model to an infinite horizon and replacing the once-for-all procedure by a period-by-period voting, the main results will change. Under these circumstances each individual will favor a tax policy that maximizes present utility. Thus, if tax effects differ with age, each voter will vote for that tax policy being optimal at that point in time.

Thereby, without redistributive pension payments (Case 1) a young voter with large inheritance expectation might even favor moderate or high taxes on wealth transfers. Although these will harm her in the future, labor tax allowances appear more appealing in the present. Given that a referendum is held in every period, such short-term voting behavior is due to the fact that tax rates are considered to underlie continuous re-optimization. The decisive voter then considers having the opportunity to vote twice in lifetime and being able to change her political decision in the future. Under imperfect policy commitment present tax effects become increasingly important. As long as population growth is positive, it hence leads to higher bequest taxes in equilibrium. However, compared to the redistributive policy in Case 2 period-by-period voting will not change optimal tax policy. This is owed to the assumption that additional inheritance taxes are levied and pension payments are redistributed within the same generation only. Thus, short-term preferences do not make any difference here.

Generally, it can be stated: as long as tax effects on the different age cohorts vary and the median voter is a young individual, then bequest tax preferences are higher, the more often tax policy is expected to be revised. In such short-term voting the median chooses an estate tax rate higher than individually optimal over time. Given that such voting structure is continued period by period, the long-term optimal tax plan is time-inconsistent.

These findings imply that short election periods, which can be observed in most modern democracies, promote a policy that overtaxes wealth transfers. In every ballot, there is a majority of individuals, currently not involved in a wealth transfer process (neither by bequeathing nor by inheriting), favoring a tax on inheritances in order to reduce the remaining tax rates or to increase redistribution.

4.4 Concluding remarks

There is ongoing political debate on the justification of wealth transfer taxes. Given that in many industrialized countries such taxation of inheritances is solely levied on the very rich, many supporters argue with redistributive reasons. According to them the taxation of intergenerational transfers leads to enhanced equity and hence to higher average standards of living. However, normative analysis shows that a taxation of bequests is welfare increasing if and only if redistributive effects are larger than the distortive effects on the affected. This holds for low inheritance tax rates only.

This chapter has explored an alternative line of thought, which emphasizes the political decision process on inheritance taxation. Observing that the tax preferences of the median voter may be contrary to normative implications, I have been endeavoring to reveal, why many countries still levy relatively high bequest taxes at least on the wealthy.

The results of the numerical analysis indicate that wealth heterogeneity may create a constituency of the poor and of those exhibiting a high 'labor income to inherited wealth' ratio to favor bequest taxation, and that redistribution of tax revenues may create a further enlarged electorate in support of taxing wealth transfers.

As a result, individual bequest tax preferences (and associated pension payments) can be supposed to crucially depend on age as well as on relative wealth and income. These numerical findings coincide with empirical evidence observed in many western democracies. To name only a few, Perotti (1996) shows that the demographic composition of the population is responsible for public spending and especially for pension expenditures, which are increasing with wealth inequality. Tabellini (2000) further reveals a positive correlation between the 'Gini index' and public transfers in a large sample of countries, controlling for age and initial income. The influence of wealth heterogeneity on voters' preferences for redistribution, has also been analyzed by Boeri, Börsch-Supan and Tabellini (2001), using opinion polls. They show that among five-thousand European citizens, the individual willingness to opt out of a pay-as-you-go pension system is systematically related to age and income, where younger and richer individuals tend to oppose to a redistributive pension system.

Hence, wealth inequality – in the sense of lower median relative to mean wealth – can be associated with higher taxation and a willingness to enlarge redistribution programs. Whereas in economic equilibrium only the average magnitudes matter, wealth heterogeneity decisively affects political majority decisions as it changes the median voter. This difference might explain why in many countries, inheritance tax rates are higher than normatively implied. The taxation of wealth transfers may hence rather be motivated by the maximization of political support than by economic optimality.

However, since political equilibria rely on constantly changing parameters, attention should be paid to changing age and wealth patterns as well as to the political environment. Current developments, like continuing aging of population or increasing international tax competition (especially among neighboring countries), will increase the influence of old and wealthy voters. Yet in the future, the political support for wealth transfer taxation might fall.

5 Wealth transfer taxation in practice: a descriptive analysis

"Governments likely to confiscate wealth are unlikely to have much wealth to confiscate in the long run."

Thomas Sowell

The preceding chapters have given normative and positive implications for the optimal taxation of bequests, summarizing literature on common bequest motives and evolving new aspects for wealth transfers of the very rich. On the basis of these criteria this chapter briefly analyzes and assesses current bequest tax systems of selected industrialized countries. It can be shown that the application of wealth transfer taxes is still persistent in many western democracies, however, tax design varies widely, and latest tax reforms exhibit a decreasing trend in wealth transfer taxation (Table 5.1).

Figure 5.1: Current top marginal tax rates on wealth transfers of selected OECD countries

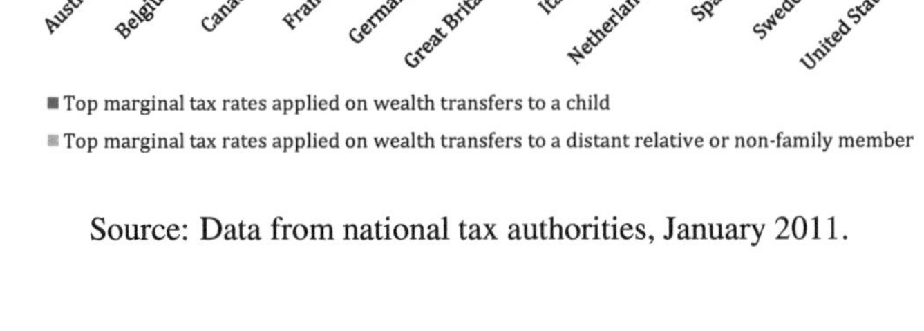

Source: Data from national tax authorities, January 2011.

In order to evaluate bequest tax design, a brief review of the existing shapes of wealth transfer taxation in selected OECD countries is given. Therein, special attention is paid to German inheritance tax law. Finally a short outlook to current reform activities is provided.

5.1 Wealth transfer taxation in the OECD countries

Generally, there are two types of wealth transfer taxes at death – whereas in some nations the testator is levied by wealth transfer taxes directly, in others it is the recipient who is charged. In the former case the tax basis is determined by the total amount of wealth bequeathed, while in the latter it is the wealth received by each heir. Whether a tax on bequests is levied in one way or another, can be regionally and historically distinguished.[80]

Among the thirty-four OECD countries, solely the United States and the United Kingdom apply estate tax systems, whereas the majority of OECD countries levies inheritance taxes. Nine countries – Australia, Austria, Canada, Israel, Mexico, New Zealand, Portugal, the Slovak Republic, and Sweden – impose neither an inheritance nor an estate tax.[81]

The **estate tax** applied in the Anglo-American area, which sometimes also is referred to as 'death tax', is organized as a uniform tax charged on the total taxable testator's wealth. Except for the own spouse who is exempted from taxation, any kinship relations between testator and heir are entirely negligible. In the *United States* the estate tax rate progressively increases with the bequest amount, currently ranging between 18 and 35 percent. Further, each taxpayer enjoys a personal tax exemption of 5,000,000 US-dollars. Estates larger than this tax exemption are subject to estate taxation, whereby only the exceeding amount is levied.[82] In the *United Kingdom*, however, each intergenerational wealth transfer is granted a certain tax exemption, which since 2009 amounts 325,000 British pounds – approximately 370,000 Euro. Bequests exceeding this exemption limit are levied by a proportional tax rate of 40 percent.[83] This uniform estate taxation usually includes no 'law of descent and distribution' which would confer rights of inheritance on blood relatives. Hence, allowing testators complete freedom to dispose

[80] For a closer examination of this development see Pestieau (2003).

[81] In Australia, Canada, and Mexico, wealth transfers, however, are treated as labor or capital income which is taxed accordingly. See Section 5.4.

[82] See Internal Revenue Service, United States (2011).

[83] Even though the taxation of wealth transfers in the UK is called 'inheritance tax' it is levied on personal representatives, and is therefore an estate tax. See Inland Revenues, United Kingdom (2011).

their wealth to anyone, not even the closest relatives are entitled to receive any share of bequeathed wealth and can be disinherited completely.

In most countries of continental Europe, on the other hand, bequests are taxed in form of a differentiated **inheritance tax**, which in contrast to the estate tax, is levied on the wealth received by the heirs. Such taxation offers the opportunity to consider family connections between testator and inheritor. In doing so, most European states bestow individual tax exemptions that depend on the degree of kinship relations (Table 5.1).

Table 5.1: Tax exemption amounts of selected European countries

Exemptions given to... (in EUR)	BE*	DE	ES	FR	IT	NL	CH
Spouses	15,000	500,000	15,957	*exempted*	1 mill.	600,000	*exempted*
Children	15,000	400,000	15,957	156,359	1 mill.	19,000	*exempted***
Others	1,250	20,000	0	1,520	0	2,000	6,529***

* for the region of Brussels

** in almost all Swiss cantons except Appenzell Innerrhoden, Neuenburg, and Waadt

*** approx. value; maximum exemption of all Swiss cantons granted in the canton of Bern

Source: Data from national tax authorities, January 2011.

Moreover, inheritance taxes in all these countries are levied double progressively, with tax rates increasing with declining degree of relationship as well as with increasing value of wealth inherited. Even though the tax structure is quite similar in all European countries, specific inheritance tax design, however, varies widely (Table 5.2). In Belgium and Switzerland, for example, an inheritance tax is paid to the regions or cantons, which each set their own tax rates and thereby cause interregional tax competition.[84] In France, the Netherlands, Spain and Germany

[84] See Administration de la Trésorerie, Belgium (2011) and Eidgenössische Steuerverwaltung, Switzerland (2011).

inheritance taxes are levied on a national level.[85] Italy, which already abolished wealth transfer taxes in 2002, reinstated inheritance taxes in 2006, but with large exemption levels and very low tax rates.[86]

Table 5.2: Inheritance tax rates of selected European countries

Entry and top tax rates (%) applied on inheritances to		BE*	DE	ES	FR	IT	NL	CH***
Spouses	min	3	7	7.65	0	4	5	0
	max	30	30	40.8	0	4	23	0
Children	min	3	7	7.65	5	4	5	0**
	max	30	30	40.8	40	4	23	0**
Others	min	40	30	15.3	60	8	41	1
	max	80	50	81.6	60	8	68	50

* for the region of Brussels

** in almost all Swiss cantons except Appenzell Innerrhoden, Neuenburg, and Waadt

*** minimum and maximum values of all Swiss cantons

Source: Data from national tax authorities, January 2011.

In contrast to the estate tax, all these differentiated tax systems in general restrict the freedom to bequeath by a specific intestate succession law. Even though the specific form differs between the nations, such law basically defines the line of succession and limits the possibilities of disinheritance. Heirs are therein classified by their relationship to the deceased, so that direct relatives (spouses, children, and grandchildren) are the first to inherit, followed by the parents and their issues (the brother or sister, nieces, and nephews) up to grandparents and their descendants (uncles, aunts, and cousins).

[85] See Administration Fiscale: Ministère de l'Économie, des Finances et de l'Industrie, France (2011), Rijksoverheid, Netherlands (2011), Ministerio de Economía y Hacienda, Spain (2011), and Bundesministerium der Finanzen, Germany (2011).

[86] See Ministero dell'Economia e delle Finanze, Italy (2011).

5.2 Inheritance taxation in Germany

Germany faces a long tradition of wealth transfer taxation. Back in the 9th century, landlords were collecting tributes for changes in ownership, called *customs on death.* The foundation to current inheritance tax law was laid by Prussian bequest tax at the end of the 19th century. Today, legislative power resides with the federation; the revenues, however, accrue to the German federal states. During its entire existence, German inheritance tax law has undergone various legislative reforms. Initiated by a verdict of the Federal Constitutional Court, the latest reform was agreed in 2009.[87]

Concentrating on those characteristics which are important for the normative and positive assessment, the following analysis solely provides a brief overview of the German inheritance tax law, in order to identify,

- who is going to be taxed,
- by which means the value of bequeathed assets is determined, as well as
- how the individual tax burden is finally calculated.

According to German inheritance tax law, each individual receiving a positive intra- and intergenerational wealth transfer is subject to inheritance taxation at the time of the testator's death. In order to determine the taxable value of inheritances, the amount bequeathed, however, has to be reduced by liabilities directly associated with the decedent's estate (e.g. funeral expenses). Thereby the net wealth transfer is identified, from which further tax exemptions of single assets and personal tax reliefs are deducted. Finally, the *taxable acquisition* is calculated on which the inheritance tax is applied (Table 5.3).

Table 5.3: Determination of the taxable value for German inheritance tax

	contribution's value (gross accretion)
-	liabilities of the estate
=	net wealth (net accretion)
-	personal and specific exemptions
=	taxable acquisition

[87] See Bundesverfassungsgericht (2007).

Personal exemptions, reducing the taxable value of wealth transfers, rest upon family relations between testator and heir. Therefore inheritors are categorized according to three tax classes:

- Class I contains spouses, children, and stepchildren as well as grandchildren, parents and grandparents.
- Class II includes siblings (also half-siblings) and their children, stepparents, parents-in-law, and divorced spouses.
- Class III subsumes all remaining heirs.

Accordingly, each heir obtains a personal tax relief, reaching from 500,000 Euro for spouses, 400,000 Euro for children, stepchildren and grandchildren, 200,000 Euro for grandchildren whose parents are still alive, 100,000 Euro for parents and grandparents, to 20,000 Euro for anyone else. Generally, testamentary freedom is granted in Germany. However, if the deceased has left a will disinheriting his spouse or close relatives by blood these would be entitled a compulsory share, which amounts to half the legal share the disinherited individual would get in an intestate succession.

German inheritance tax law further grants *specific exemptions* for real estates and business property. This special treatment has undergone a series of changes in the latest inheritance tax reform, reducing tax liabilities on specific assets transferred to closest relatives. Thereby, for example, the inheritance of a family home is simplified which, under certain conditions, may remain entirely untaxed. Moreover, heirs of domestic family enterprises recently are able choose between two regulations, which, among other restrictions, oblige the heir to continue the business for seven or ten years, so that at best the inheritance of a family enterprise is not subject to wealth transfer taxation at all.

After deducting these tax exemptions, the remaining taxable value is levied by double progressive tax rates which increase with the amount of wealth inherited as well as with diminishing degree of relationship between testator and heir (Table 5.4).

As a result, German inheritance tax law exhibits a rather complex evaluation method. Due to vast exemption levels, a wide majority of bequests remains untaxed, whereas transfers which exceed personal or specific tax exemptions are taxed rather significantly. In consequence tax revenues are quite low, whereas the tax burden of those affected is clearly noticeable.

Within the last decade, annual inheritance tax revenues have varied between 3.0 and 4.2 billion Euro, generating less than one percent of total tax revenues (Table 5.5).

Table 5.4: Inheritance tax rates according to tax classes in Germany

taxable value up to... EUR (until 2008)	tax rates in tax classes (until 2008)		
	I	II	III
75,000 (52,000)	7 (7)	30 (12)	30 (17)
300,000 (256,000)	11 (11)	30 (17)	30 (23)
600,000 (512,000)	15 (15)	30 (22)	30 (29)
6,000,000 (5,113,000)	19 (19)	30 (27)	30 (35)
13,000,000 (12,783,000)	23 (23)	50 (32)	50 (41)
26,000,000 (25,565,000)	27 (27)	50 (37)	50 (47)
>26,000,000 (>25,565,000)	30 (30)	50 (40)	50 (50)

Source: Data from Bundesministerium der Finanzen, Germany (2011).

Table 5.5: Inheritance tax revenues in Germany between 2003 and 2009

year	2003	2004	2005	2006	2007	2008	2009*
Inheritance tax revenues (in million EUR)	2,968	3,769	3,605	3,311	3,699	4,199	4,004*
... as a share of total revenues (in %)	0.39	0.49	0.46	0.40	0.42	0.46	0.45*

* estimated value

Source: Data from OECD Statistics (2011); own calculations.

By international comparison Germany therewith aligns below-average, given that inheritance tax revenues as a share of total revenues in the OECD countries vary between 0.02 percent (in Italy) and 2.25 percent (in Japan).[88]

[88] See OECD (2009).

The analysis of the taxpayers' composition reveals that the majority of the inheritance tax burden is born by a small number of recipients of large wealth transfers. Translated into figures, 23.7 percent of the annual revenues are generated by those individuals receiving an inheritance of five million Euro and above. In relative terms, these constitute solely 0.28 percent of all wealth transfers realized within one year. Recipients of inheritances above 2.5 million Euro already produce 31.8 percent of bequest tax revenues. However, accounting for 0.71 percent of total wealth transfers, they likewise carry no significant numerical weight. In consequence, approximately three-quarters of German inheritance tax revenues are generated by a tenth of all wealth transfers, exhibiting a taxable wealth of more than 200,000 Euro.[89]

5.3 Assessment of current bequest tax policy

The choice of one form of wealth transfer tax system over another necessarily involves trade-offs among efficiency, equity, and political feasibility. A determination whether one system is preferable to another can be made on the basis of each system's success in achieving one or a majority of these goals, without excessively sacrificing the achievement of the others.

Regardless of whether the tax is imposed on the deceased or the heir, one may assert that the economic burden of both approaches always falls on the heirs, as the amount received is effectively reduced by the amount of taxes paid, no matter by whom.[90] On the other hand, one may argue that an inheritance tax is more effective in encouraging dispersal of wealth among a greater number of heirs and potentially to lower-income beneficiaries, promoting fairness in the tax system.[91]

Thus, assessing the characteristics of European inheritance taxes and Anglo-American estate taxes according to the aspects of optimal wealth transfer taxation evolved in the preceding chapters of this study, it can be stated that in regard to **normative** criteria inheritance tax in general takes greater account to individual bequest motives than a uniform estate tax. Applying differentiated exemption levels and lower tax rates on direct relatives, the inheritance tax usually privileges dynastic bequests. In contrary, the existence of low exemption levels and high tax rates applied to distant relatives or non-family members is based on the assumption that these inheritances are mostly unintended and thus are justifiably exposed to high taxation. Due to highly progressive tax rates, however, wealth transfers of the

[89] See Statistisches Bundesamt (2010).
[90] See Batchelder (2007).
[91] See Scheffler and Wigger (2006).

very rich, even to close family members, underlie excessive taxation. According to the normative implications evolved for capitalistic bequests such taxation may create inefficiencies which, in regard to social welfare, shall be avoided.

Evaluating inheritance and estate taxes on the basis of the afore defined **positive** criteria, the inheritance tax again reveals to be closer to political-economic considerations, providing an explanation for high top rates applied even on close relatives. It can be argued that excessive taxation of large transfers describes a majoritarian desire of those societies characterized by inequality. Reflecting the political result of collective choice processes, high tax rates on the very rich may thus be optimal in order to gain political majorities, since the recipients of redistributive politics outnumber the affected heirs of large inheritances. Political majorities, however, are subject to constantly changing parameters, so that current developments, like continuing aging of population or increasing international tax competition, in the future may change political equilibria towards those affected by bequest taxation.

Yet, looking at the inheritance tax more closely – on the example of current tax law in Germany – many of the normative criteria of optimal bequest taxation are incorporated. In this regard, extensions of personal tax relief aim to reduce tax evasion. Also a steeper progression in tax classes II and III, may further intend to levy higher taxes on those bequests indicating to be unplanned.

The inclusion of a 'capitalist spirit' and thereby the accounting for specific preferences of very wealthy individuals, however, is less evident in Germany analog to many other European countries. Even though current law already pays increased attention to a growing political weight of wealthy individuals by raising personal tax reliefs for direct relatives as well as by easing the tax burden on intergenerational transfers of family-run enterprises, bequest taxes applied on the very wealthy are still considerably high.

Generally, the majority of inheritances in Germany does not underlie taxation at all. This is due to the fact that most wealth transfers are relatively small and exemption levels and personal tax reliefs are high. However, heirs of very large assets, independent of their degree of kinship, are subject to excessive taxation, so that even closest relatives are encouraged to avoid taxation. An international comparison reveals that, due to these characteristics, Germany's competitiveness with regard to wealth transfer taxation solely can be rated in the mid-field. Whereas in other nations spouses and sometimes even children are entirely exempted from taxes on wealth transfers, Germany levies significant tax rates on those amounts exceeding tax exemptions.[92] Such differences can be supposed to receive greater importance with growing tax competition among the nations.

Even though inheritance taxation reveals a better compliance with theoretical implications, it has to be taken into account that, due to its variety of specific regulations, it is rather complex in its evaluation method and quite costly in its implementation.

During the last few years many OECD countries have been showing **signs of reforming** their wealth transfer tax system. Table 5.6 provides a brief overview on recent estate as well as inheritance tax reforms. The overall tendency is declining, characterized by either a raise in personal tax allowances and a reduction in overall tax rates or even a complete abolishment.

Most recently, in December 2010, the US passed a law exempting estates smaller than 5 million US-dollars from the federal estate tax, and creating a maximum estate tax rate of 35 percent. Previously, the American estate tax had undergone a series of changes and had been exposed to ongoing discussion. Personal tax exemption amounts were raised from 1.5 to 2 million US-dollars in 2006 and again to 3.5 million US-dollars in 2009. Under the former president Bush a law was enacted repealing the federal estate tax in 2010. This abolishment for the duration of one year was made with the intention to relaunch the estate tax at the beginning of 2011 – applying personal tax exemptions of 1 million US-dollars and tax rates that were valid in 2001.[93] Although the federal estate tax was officially repealed on January 1, 2010, President Obama signed a 'Tax Relief Act' into law on December 2010, which reinstated the estate tax retroactively back to the beginning of 2010 and also set new rules for the estates of decedents dying in 2011 and 2012.[94] This law, however, is only valid until December 31, 2012, so that in 2013 the estate tax law will either revert back to that effective in 2001 or will be redesigned once again.

In order to complete the descriptive analysis of current wealth transfer taxation, I would like to point out that among the OECD countries some nations do not impose a separate tax on bequests, but instead treat wealth transfers either as gross income of the recipients or as capital gains realized by the deceased. Such **alternatives** to wealth transfer taxation are imposed in Canada, Australia, and Mexico.

[92]For example, in Great Britain, Ireland, Denmark, the US, Japan as well as in most parts of Switzerland and Luxembourg spouses remain completely untaxed. Bequests to the own children are further tax exempted in Luxembourg and a majority of Swiss cantons. See Scheffler and Spengel (2004).

[93]In 2001 tax rates varied between 18 and 55 percent. Hence, compared to 2009, estate tax law would have been significantly tightened, with lower exemptions and higher top rates.

[94]See One Hundred Eleventh Congress of the United States of America (2010).

Table 5.6: Recent wealth transfer tax reforms in selected OECD countries

	year	major changes
Austria	2008	*abolished*
Belgium	2007	complete tax exemption for family companies in Flanders
France	2007	complete tax exemption of surviving spouses higher exemptions for all other recipients
Germany	2009	higher exemptions to close relatives higher entry and top tax rates for tax classes II and III option: tax-free business succession for family-run companies
Italy	2007	reinstated with significant lower rates and higher exemptions
Netherlands	2010	lower rates and reduced number of tariff categories higher exemptions business succession facilitated
Portugal	2004	*abolished*
Spain	2010	tax exemptions gradually increase until July 2011 lower tax rates, except for distant relatives
Sweden	2005	*abolished*
United Kingdom	2007	gradual increase of exemptions until 2010-11
United States	2010	higher exemptions lower top rates

Source: Data from national tax authorities, January 2011.

Under an *income inclusion approach*, bequests in Mexico generally are treated as income of the recipients and are thereby subject to income taxation. The inheritance is cumulated with the heir's other income and reported on the annual income tax return, so that intergenerational wealth transfers are taxed under the same rate schedule applicable to the taxpayer's remaining income. Australia and Canada, on the other hand, regard bequests as capital gains, using a *deemed-realization rule*. At death, the decedent is considered to have disposed of capital assets at fair market value and all gains are reported on her final income tax return. In general, the tax rates applied to gains on deemed-realizations, resulting from bequests, correspond to those on regular capital gains.

Whether these systems are superior to the classical wealth transfer tax systems, which tax either estates or inheritances detached from decedent's or heir's income, has not been examined in this study. However, they might provide an alternative as possible replacements for current transfer taxes.

6 Conclusion

6.1 Results of this study

Answering *"How to optimally tax capitalistic bequests?"* this thesis was concerned with the impact of wealth transfer taxation on economic as well as on political equilibria. Optimality conditions were analyzed regarding the specific preferences of very rich individuals – intending to either minimize inefficiencies and enhance redistribution or to gain political majorities.

Although the analyzed economic environments can solely describe a stylized representation of reality, the gained findings provide important implications for optimal bequest tax design.

Empirical evidence implies that real-world bequest taxes in general are mostly levied on very wealthy testators or their descendants. In addition Hurd (1987), Laitner and Juster (1996), and De Nardi (2004) find that these individuals dedicate wealth to guarantee the continuance of lifetime achievements beyond own death and thus try to avoid any tax-induced reduction in personal wealth.

In accordance to these studies, I have laid down that the specific preference structure of rich individuals incorporates decisive implications for mitigating tax induced distortions and at the same time enhancing redistribution. Further, it influences the overall political feasibility of bequest tax policy. In particular, the impact of a 'capitalist spirit' proves to be sensitive to bequest taxation, inducing behavioral changes or even tax avoidance activities of very wealthy individuals. The understanding of this different behavior is essential in order to assess economic and political effects of wealth transfer taxation and to optimize fiscal policy decisions.

The analysis of common bequest motives – like altruism, paternalism, or strategic intention – induces that optimal bequest tax design should be orientated towards the underlying transfer motive each deceased pursues when bequeathing wealth. However, I have shown that none of these universal bequest motives has revealed to be an effective explanation for capitalist's saving and wealth transfer behavior. Consequently, neither normative nor positive implications for the optimal wealth transfer taxation of the very rich have been explored in existing literature. Therefore I have evolved a 'capitalist spirit' model in which wealthy individuals are assumed to gain additional utility directly by holding assets and by passing wealth to following generations. On the basis of this capitalistic bequest motive a normative and positive analysis of wealth transfers is implemented within a society heterogeneous in age and wealth, intending to reveal reliable implications for optimal bequest tax design.

Normative analysis implies that behavioral effects released on a rich individual when being taxed, depend on the intensity of the 'capitalist spirit' and on the amount of wealth the individual holds. It could be laid down that the more intense this 'capitalist spirit', the higher bequests and the smaller behavioral changes, but the more frequent are tax avoidance methods. Contrasting, it could be shown that the smaller the individual's personal wealth, the smaller are capitalistic savings and bequests, which become even less valuable when wealth transfers are intended to be taxed in the future. This induces that the smaller capitalistic savings the more sensitive individuals are to wealth transfer taxation.

Based on these effects observed for individual's capitalistic utility, social welfare implications suggest a low or moderate bequest taxation of the very wealthy's transfers. Applied supplementary to labor income taxation, bequest taxes on capitalistic wealth transfers may thereby enhance overall welfare, when incorporating both the distortive and the redistributive effects triggered in a society which is heterogeneous in age and wealth. Nonetheless, with imposing taxes on personal wealth, tax avoidance methods of the affected become rather attractive. I have therefore allowed for the existence of tax-privileged charitable foundations, resulting in a complete shift of very rich individuals' bequests to an own foundation, reducing dynastic bequests to zero. An evaluation of associated social welfare effects reveals ambiguous results, since it enhances welfare by charitable giving but entirely withdraws intergenerational wealth transfers within the families. Hence, based on these results, an excessive bequest taxation forcing the wealthy to form an own charitable foundation cannot be assessed to concurrently enhance social welfare.

By providing insights into the political decision process on wealth transfer taxation, *positive* analysis has supposed that tax preferences of the median voter may be contrary to normative implications. Using a numerical simulation, I have shown that wealth heterogeneity creates a constituency of the poor and of those exhibiting a high ratio of 'own labor income to inherited wealth' to favor bequest taxation. An additional redistribution of tax revenues has further revealed an even enlarged electorate in support of taxing capitalistic wealth transfers. These results emerge from the fact that wealth heterogeneity decisively affects political majorities as it changes the median voter. Thus, individuals benefiting from taxation may dominate those affected, inducing higher tax rates than normatively optimal. My analysis has shown that these political equilibria, however, rely on constantly changing parameters, so that attention must be paid to changing age and wealth patterns as well as to the political environment.

Even though normative and positive analysis in general lead to quite different results, both provide a sound explanation as to why many countries continue to levy bequest taxes at least on the wealthy. Nonetheless, in almost all western democracies an inclusion of a 'capitalist spirit' and thereby the accounting for specific preferences of very wealthy individuals is less evident. Bequest tax policy has concentrated rather on consanguinity, incorporating the idea of family-oriented bequests, than on testamentary decrees. For a capitalist, however, a will may even stand for choosing the best alternative satisfying the continuation process of own wealth in the future. During the last few years, current bequest tax policy in many OECD countries has exhibited various signs of reforming. The overall tendency can be described in a declining importance of wealth transfer tax revenues, characterized by either a raise in personal tax allowances and a reduction in overall tax rates or even a complete abolishment.

Altogether, supplementary to existing literature on family-oriented bequests, the results derived in this thesis, propose that optimal bequest tax policy shall pay attention to the unique characteristics of the very wealthy's preferences. Such policy may be advantageous in order to reduce tax avoidance and thereby create additional tax revenues – not only from wealth transfers but also from other types of taxes.

6.2 Policy recommendations

This study has dealt with the taxation of capitalistic bequests and has therewith concentrated on those few wealthy individuals who actually owe wealth transfer taxes at death. As tax theory suggests, tax design should always incorporate the elasticities of the assets taxed, implying that in case of wealth transfer taxation the specific characteristics of wealthy individuals should be taken into account. Even though the theoretical results evolved throughout this study naturally cannot depict a universal, 'best and only' bequest tax system, they nevertheless can arise important implications for bequest tax design.

One the one hand, negative economic consequences induced by excessive wealth transfer taxation, should be faced by lowering top rates and broadening the tax basis in order to guarantee welfare-increasing redistribution.[95] Those recipients appointed by will shall further be granted tax reductions, in order to give even more weight to the bequest motivation of the deceased. Implementation, on the other hand, further indicates a bequest taxation of the wealthy is barely feasible, as long as rich individuals strive to avoid taxation. A greater flexibility in work arrangements as well as sophistication in financial advice and options available, facilitate the wealthy to respond much stronger to taxation than average individuals. These tax avoidance methods ultimately raise the social cost per unit of revenue actually collected.

Hence, there appears to be a conceptual distinction of whether the rich *should* and whether they *can* be taxed excessively – an indication for the problematic feasibility of wealth transfer taxation. Changing conditions in the economic environment – e.g. freedom of movement, right of establishment, and freedom to provide services within the European Union – additionally enhance tax avoidance opportunities. To counter this, nations already compete for wealthy individuals. Many western countries have recently either abolished wealth transfers taxation or reduced tax rates and raised exemption levels. They are aware that rich individuals are more likely to promote a higher capital accumulation and thereby an increasing welfare in the long-run.

Creating a wealth transfer tax without loopholes is difficult for administrative reasons. However, it is sensible to ask, whether the bequest tax's advantages of facilitating redistribution and its disadvantages of encouraging tax avoidance might be better balanced in a tax system that pays attention to capitalistic bequests. This study suggests that the characteristic preferences of rich individuals differ considerably and proposes their consideration in bequest tax design. Political decision makers should aim for a tax system that causes voluntary tax discipline – even of the wealthiest families. Recent bequest tax legislation in many industrialized countries hence invites further reform of wealth transfer taxation to mitigate its problems but to retain its advantages.

[95] It is argued that wealth tax would need to be confiscatory in order to bring about any real redistribution. See Heckly (2004).

Bibliography

Aaron, H. J. and Munnell, A. H. (1992), Reassessing the Role for Wealth Transfer Taxes, *National Tax Journal*, 45 (2), 119–143.

Abel, A. B. (1985), Precautionary Saving and Accidental Bequests, *American Economic Review*, 75 (4), 777–791.

Abel, A. B. and Warshawsky, M. (1988), Specification of the Joy of Giving: Insights from Altruism, *The Review of Economics and Statistics*, 70 (4), 145–150.

Administration de la Trésorerie, Belgium (2011), Ministry of Revenue or Taxation: http://www.treasury.fgov.be.

Administration Fiscale: Ministère de l'Économie, des Finances et de l'Industrie, France (2011), Ministry of Revenue or Taxation: http://www.impots.gouv.fr.

Andreoni, J. (1989), Giving with Impure Altruism: Applications to Charity and Ricardian Equivalence, *Journal of Political Economy*, 97 (6), 1447–1458.

Arrondel, L. and Laferrère, A. (2001), Taxation and Wealth Transmission in France, *Journal of Public Economics*, 79 (1), 3–33.

Atkinson, A. B. (1980), Inheritance and the Redistribution of Wealth, in: Heal, G. M. and Hughes, G. A., editors, Public policy and the tax system, London: Allen and Unwin.

Atkinson, A. B. (1981), The Economics of Inequality, Oxford: Clarendon Press.

Atkinson, A. B. and Sandmo, A. (1980), Welfare Implications of the Taxation of Savings, *The Economic Journal*, 90, 529–549.

Atkinson, A. B. and Stiglitz, J. E. (1980), Lectures on Public Economics, London: McGraw-Hill International Editions.

Auerbach, A. J. (1985), The Theory of the Excess Burden and Optimal Taxation, in: Auerbach, A. J. and Feldstein, M., editors, Handbook of Public Economics, Vol.1, North-Holland: Elsevier, 69–127.

Aura, S. (2004), Estate and Capital Gains Taxation: Efficiency and Political Economy Considerations, CESifo Group Munich – CESifo Working Paper Series.

Bakija, J. and Slemrod, J. (2004), Do the Rich flee from high State Taxes?: Evidence from Federal Estate Tax Returns, National Bureau of Economic Research – NBER Working Papers.

Bakija, J. M., Gale, W. G. and Slemrod, J. B. (2003), Charitable Bequests and Taxes on Inheritances and Estates: Aggregate Evidence from across States and Time, *American Economic Review*, 93 (2), 366–370.

Barro, R. J. (1974), Are Government Bonds Net Wealth, *Journal of Political Economy*, 82, 1095–1117.

Barro, R. J. and Friedman, J. W. (1977), On Uncertain Lifetimes, *Journal of Political Economy*, 85 (4), 843–849.

Batchelder, L. (2007), Taxing Privilege More Effectively: Replacing the Estate Tax with an Inheritance Tax, NYU Law and Economics Research Paper No. 07-25 – Hamilton Project Discussion Paper.

Becker, G. S. (1974), A Theory of Social Interactions, *Journal of Political Economy*, 84 (6), 1063–1093.

Becker, G. S. (1983), A Theory of Competition Among Pressure Groups for Political Influence, *The Quarterly Journal of Economics*, 98 (3), 371–400.

Becker, G. S. (1985), Public Policies, Pressure Groups, and Dead Weight Costs, *Journal of Public Economics*, 28 83), 329–347.

Becker, G. S. and Tomes, N. (1979), An Equilibrium Theory of the Distribution of Income and Intergenerational Mobility, *Journal of Political Economy*, 87, 1153–1189.

Bernheim, B. D. (1999), Taxation and Saving, National Bureau of Economic Research – NBER Working Papers.

Bernheim, B. D., Shleifer, A. and Summers, L. H. (1985), The Strategic Bequest Motive, *Journal of Political Economy*, 93 (6), 1045–1076.

Bertocchi, G. (2007), The Vanishing Bequest Tax: The Comparative Evolution of Bequest Taxation in Historical Perspective, Institute for the Study of Labor (IZA) (2578). – IZA Discussion Papers.

Black, D. (1958), Theory of Committees and Elections, Cambridge, UK: Cambridge University Press.

Blinder, A. S. (1976), Intergenerational Transfers and Life Cycle Consumption, *American Economic Review, Papers and Proceedings*, 66, 87–93.

Blumkin, T. and Sadka, E. (2003), Estate Taxation with Intended and Accidental Bequests, *Journal of Public Economics*, 88, 1–21.

Boeri, T., Börsch-Supan, A. and Tabellini, G. (2001), Would you like to Shrink the Welfare State? A Survey of European Citizens, *Economic Policy*, 16 (32), 7–50.

Bohn, H. (1991), Endogenous Government Spending and Ricardian Equivalence, *The Economic Journal*, 102 (412), 588–597.

Brennan, G. and Buchanan, J. M. (1977), Towards a Tax Constitution for Leviathan, *Journal of Public Economics*, 8 (3), 255–273.

Breyer, F. and Ursprung, H. W. (1998), Are the Rich Too Rich to be Expropriated?: Economic Power and the Feasibility of Constitutional Limits to Redistribution, *Public Choice*, 94 (1-2), 135–156.

Bruce, N. and Waldman, M. (1990), The Rotten-Kid Theorem Meets the Samaritan's Dilemma, *The Quarterly Journal of Economics*, 105 (1), 155–165.

Buchanan, J.M. (1976), Taxation in Fiscal Exchange, *Journal of Public Economics*, 6, 17–29.

Bundesministerium der Finanzen, Germany (2011), Ministry of Revenue or Taxation: http://bundesfinanzministerium.de.

Bundesverfassungsgericht (2007), Pressemitteilung Nr.11/2007 - 31.Januar 2007, Karlsruhe.

Carroll, C. D. (1998), Why do the Rich Save so Much? National Bureau of Economic Research – NBER Working Papers.

Chamley, C. (1986), Optimal Taxation of Capital Income in General Equilibrium with Infinite Lives, *Econometrica*, 54 (3), 607–622.

Cigno, A. (1993), Intergenerational Transfers without Altruism : Family, Market and State, *European Journal of Political Economy*, 9, 505–518.

Coughlin, P. J., Mueller, D. C. and Murrell, P. (1990), A Model of Electoral Competition with Interest Groups, *Economic Letters*, 32, 307–311.

Cox, D. (1987), Motives for Private Income Transfers, *Journal of Political Economy*, 95 (3), 508–546.

Cremer, H. and Pestieau, P. (2006), Wealth Transfer Taxation: A Survey of the Theoretical Literature, in: Kolm, S.C. and Mercier Ythier, J., editors, Handbook of the Economics of Giving, Altruism and Reciprocity, North Holland: Elsevier, 1107–1134.

Davies, J. B. (1981), Uncertain Lifetime, Life Insurance and Dissaving in Retirement, *Journal of Political Economy*, 89, 561–577.

Davies, J. B. and Shorrocks, A. F. (2000), The Distribution of Wealth, in: Atkinson, A. B. and Bourguignon, F., editors, Handbook of Income Distribution, Vol.1, Elsevier, Amsterdam, 605–675.

De Nardi, M. (2004), Wealth Inequality and Intergenerational Links, *Review of Economic Studies*, 71, 743–768.

Diamond, P. A. (1965), National Debt in a Neoclassical Growth Model, *American Economic Review*, 55, 1126–1150.

Donges, J. B. et al. (2007), Erbschaftsteuer: behutsam anpassen, Stiftung Marktwirtschaft (46). – Technical report.

Dworkin, R. M. (1977), Taking Rights Seriously, Cambridge, MA: Harvard University Press.

Dynan, K. E., Skinner, J. and Zeldes, S. P. (2004), Do the Rich Save More? *Journal of Political Economy*, 112 (2), 397–444.

Eidgenössische Steuerverwaltung, Switzerland (2011), Ministry of Revenue or Taxation: http://www.estv.admin.ch.

Fahri, E. and Werning, I. (2006), Progressive Estate Taxation, National Bureau of Economic Research – NBER Working Paper Series.

Francis, J. (2008), Wealth and the Capitalist Spirit, – Fordham Economics Discussion Paper Series.

Frick, J. et al. (2007), Zur Erfassung von Einkommen und Vermögen in Haushaltssurveys: Hocheinkommensstichprobe und Vermögensbilanz im SOEP, DIW, Berlin: German Socio-Economic Panel Study (19). – SOEP Papers.

Friedman, M. (1957), The Permanent Income Hypothesis, in: A Theory of the Consumption Function Princeton University Press, 20–37.

Gale, W. G. and Perozek, M. (2000), Do Estate Taxes Reduce Savings? in: Gale, W.G., Hines Jr., J. and Slemrod, J., editors, Rethinking Estate and Gift Taxation, Brookings Institution Washington D.C., 216–298.

Gale, W. G. and Scholz, J. K. (1994), Intergenerational Transfers and the Accumulation of Wealth, *Journal of Economic Perspectives*, 8 (4), 145–160.

Gale, W. G. and Slemrod, J. (2000), Overview, in: Gale, W.G., Hines Jr., J. and Slemrod, J., editors, Rethinking Estate and Gift Taxation, Brookings Institution Washington D.C., 1–64.

Geary, R. C. (1949-50), A Note on: A Constant-Utility Index of the Cost of Living, *Review of Economic Studies*, No. 18, 65–66.

Hammar, H., Jagers, S. C. and Nordblom, K. (2006), What explains Attitudes towards Tax Levels?: A Multi-Tax Comparison, Göteborg University, Department of Economics (225). – Working Papers in Economics.

Harsanyi, J. C. (1995), A Theory of Prudential Values and a Rule Utilitarian Theory of Morality, *Social Choice and Welfare*, 12 (4), 319–333.

Heckly, C. (2004), Wealth Tax in Europe: Why the Downturn? in: Taly, M. and Mestrallet, G., editors, Estate Taxation: Ideas for Reform, Institut de l'entreprise Paris, 39–50.

Hettich, W. and Winer, S. (1984), A Positive Model of Tax Structure, *Journal of Public Economics*, 24 (1), 67–87.

Hindricks, L. (2004), Accounting for Patterns of Wealth Inequality, – ASU Department of Economics Working Paper No. 8/02.

Huffman, G. W. (1996), Endogenous Tax Determination and the Distribution of Wealth, *Carnegie-Rochester Conference Series on Public Policy*, 45 (1), 207–242.

Hurd, M. D. (1987), Savings of the Elderly and Desired Bequests, *American Economic Review*, 77 (3), 298–312.

Inland Revenues, United Kingdom (2011), Ministry of Revenue or Taxation: http://www.inlandrevenue.gov.uk.

Internal Revenue Service, United States (2011), Ministry of Revenue or Taxation: http://www.irs.gov.

Joulfaian, D. (2006), Inheritance and Saving, National Bureau of Economic Research – NBER Working Papers.

Judd, K. L. (1985), Redistributive Taxation in a Simple Perfect Foresight Model, *Journal of Public Economics*, 28 (1), 59–83.

Kaplow, L. (2000), A Framework for Assessing Estate and Gift Taxation, in: Gale, W.G., Hines Jr., J. and Slemrod, J., editors, Rethinking Estate and Gift Taxation, Brookings Institution Washington D.C., 164–215.

Kopczuk, W. (2002), The Trick is to Live: Is the Estate Tax Social Security for the Rich? National Bureau of Economic Research – NBER Working Papers.

Kopczuk, W. and Lupton, J. (2007), To Leave or Not to Leave: The Distribution of Bequest Motives, *Review of Economic Studies*, 74 (1), 207–235.

Kopczuk, W. and Slemrod, J. (2000), The Impact of the Estate Tax on the Wealth Accumulation and Avoidance Behaviour of Donors, in: Gale, W.G., Hines Jr., J. and Slemrod, J., editors, Rethinking Estate and Gift Taxation, Brookings Institution Washington D.C., 299–349.

Kotlikoff, L. J. and Spivak, A. (1981), The Family as an Incomplete Annuities Market, *Journal of Political Economy*, 89 (2), 372–391.

Kotlikoff, L. J. and Summers, L. H. (1981), The Role of Intergenerational Transfers in Aggregate Capital Accumulation, *Journal of Political Economy*, 89 (4), 706–732.

Laferrere, A. (2000), Intergenerational Transmission Models: A Survey, in: Gerard-Varet, L.-A., Kolm, S.-C. and Mercier Ythier, J., editors, The Economics of Reciprocity, Giving and Altruism, International Economic Association, 207–225.

Laitner, J. and Juster, F. T. (1996), New Evidence on Altruism: A Study of TIAA-CREF Retirees, *American Economic Review*, 86 (4), 893–908.

Lindahl, E. (1919), Just Taxation: A Positive Solution, in: Musgrave, R. and Peacock, A., editors, Classics in the Theory of Public Finance, New York: Macmillan, 1958, 72–118.

Luo, Y. and Young, E. R. (2009), The Wealth Distribution And The Demand For Status, *Macroeconomic Dynamics*, 13 (S1), 1–30.

Masson, A. and Pestieau, P. (1997), Bequests Motives and Models of Inheritance: A Survey of the Literature, in: Erreygers, G. and Vandewelde, T., editors, Is Inheritance Legitimate?: Ethical and Economic Aspects of Wealth Transfers, Heidelberg: Springer Verlag, 54–88.

Mateos-Planas, X. (2010), Demographics and the Politics of Capital Taxation in a Life-Cycle Economy, *American Economic Review*, 100 (1), 337–363.

Meltzer, A. H. and Richard, S. F. (1981), A Rational Theory of the Size of Government, *Journal of Political Economy*, 89 (5), 914–927.

Michel, P. and Pestieau, P. (2004), Fiscal Policy in an Overlapping Generations Model with Bequest-As-Consumption, *Journal of Public Economic Theory*, 6 (3), 397–407.

Ministerio de Economía y Hacienda, Spain (2011), Ministry of Revenue or Taxation: http://www.meh.es.

Ministero dell'Economia e delle Finanze, Italy (2011), Ministry of Revenue or Taxation: http://www.tesoro.it.

Mirrlees, J. A. (1971), An Exploration in the Theory of Optimum Income Taxation, *Review of Economic Studies*, 38 (114), 175–208.

Modigliani, F. (1986), Life Cycle, Individual Thrift and the Wealth of Nations, *American Economic Review*, 76, 297–313.

Modigliani, F. (1988), The Role of Intergenerational Transfers and Life Cycle Saving in the Accumulation of Wealth, *Journal of Economic Perspectives*, 2 (2), 15–40.

Modigliani, F. and Brumberg, R. (1954), Utility Analysis and the Consumption Function: An Interpretation of Cross-Section Data, in: Kurihara, K., editor, Post-keynesian economics, New Brunswick.

Nordblom, K. and Ohlsson, H. (2006), Tax Avoidance and Intra-Family Transfers, *Journal of Public Economics*, 90 (8-9), 1669–1680.

OECD (2008), Growing Unequal? Income Distribution and Poverty in OECD Countries, Organisation for Economic Co-operation and Development OECD.

OECD (2009), Revenue Statistics 1965-2008, Organisation for Economic Co-operation and Development OECD.

OECD Statistics (2011), http://stats.oecd.org/, Database: Revenue Statistics - OECD Member Countries.

One Hundred Eleventh Congress of the United States of America (2010), Temporary Estate Tax Relief, http://origin.www.gpo.gov/fdsys/pkg/BILLS-111hr4853enr/pdf/BILLS-111hr4853enr.pdf.

Perotti, R. (1996), Growth, Income Distribution, and Democracy: What the Data Say, *Journal of Economic Growth*, 1 (2), 149–187.

Persson, T. and Tabellini, G. (2000), Political Economics: Explaining Economic Policy, Massachusetts: MIT Press.

Pestieau, P. (2003), The Role of Gift and Estate Transfers in the United States and in Europe, in: Munnell, A. and Sunden, A., editors, Death and Dollars - The Role of Gifts and Bequests in America, The Brookings Institution Press, Washington D.C., 64–90.

Ramsey, F. R. (1927), A Contribution to the Theory of Taxation, *The Economic Journal*, 37, 47–61.

Razin, A. and Sadka, E. (2007), Aging Population: The Complex Effect of Fiscal Leakages on the Politico-Economic Equilibrium, *European Journal of Political Economy*, 23, 564–575.

Razin, A., Sadka, E. and Swagel, P. (2002), The Aging Population and the Size of the Welfare State, *Journal of Political Economy*, 110 (4), 900–918.

Reil-Held, A. (2002), Die Rolle intergenerationaler Transfers in Einkommen und Vermögen älterer Menschen in Deutschland, Mannheimer Forschungsinstitut Ökonomie und demographischer Wandel, Universität Mannheim – MEA-Studies.

Renström, T. (1996), Endogenous Taxation: An Overlapping Generations Approach, *Economic Journal*, 106 (435), 471–482.

Richter, W. F. (1987), Taxation as Insurance and the Case of Rate Differentiation according to Consanguinity under Inheritance Taxation, *Journal of Public Economics*, 33, 363–376.

Rijksoverheid, Netherlands (2011), Ministry of Revenue or Taxation: http://www.rijksoverheid.nl.

Saez, E. (2002), Optimal Progressive Capital Income Taxes in the Infinite Horizon Model, National Bureau of Economic Research – NBER Working Papers.

Sandmo, A. (2005), The theory of Tax Evasion: A Retrospective View. *National Tax Journal*, 58, 643–663.

Scheffler, W. and Spengel, C. (2004), Erbschaftsteuerbelastung im internationalen Vergleich, Baden-Baden: Nomos Verlagsgesellschaft, ZEW Wirtschaftsanalysen, Schriftenreihe des ZEW, 75.

Scheffler, W. and Wigger, B. U. (2006), Zur geplanten Reform der Erbschaftsteuer, *Betriebs-Berater*, 45, 2443–2448.

Sexauer, M. (2004), Verteilungswirkung und Effizienz der Erbschaftsteuer - Eine Untersuchung im Rahmen von Modellen überlappender Generationen, Ph. D thesis, TU Dresden.

Slemrod, J. (1990), Optimal Taxation and Optimal Tax Systems, *Journal of Economic Perspectives*, 4, 157–178.

Slemrod, J. (2001), A General Model of the Behavioral Response to Taxation, *International Tax and Public Finance*, 8 (2), 119–128.

Statistisches Bundesamt (2010), Erbschaft- und Schenkungsteuerstatistik Deutschland 2008, Statistisches Bundesamt, Wiesbaden.

Stern, N. H. (1974), The Theory of Optimal Commodity and Income Taxation: In Introduction, in: Newbery, D. and Stern, N. H., editors, The Theory of Taxation for Developing Countries, Oxford University Press.

Stiglitz, J. E. (1978), Notes on Estate Taxes, Redistribution, and Concept of Balanced Growth Path Incidence, *Journal of Political Economy*, 86 (2), 137–150.

Stiglitz, J. E. (1987), Pareto Efficient and Optimal Taxation and the New Welfare Economics, in: Auerbach, A. and Feldstein, M., editors, Handbook of Public Economics, Vol.2, Elsevier.

Stone, R. (1954), Linear Expenditure Systems and Demand Analysis: An Application to the Pattern of British Demand, *The Economic Journal*, 64 (255), 511–527.

Szydlik, M. (2004), Inheritance and Inequality: Theoretical Reasoning and Empirical Evidence, *European Sociological Review*, 20 (1), 31–45.

Tabellini, G. (1991), The Politics of Intergenerational Redistribution, *Journal of Political Economy*, 99 (2), 335–357.

Tabellini, G. (2000), A Positive Theory of Social Security, *Scandinavian Journal of Economics*, 102 (3), 523–545.

Traxler, C. (2009), Voting over Taxes: the Case of Tax Evasion, *Public Choice*, 140 (1-2), 43–58.

Weber, M. (1905), The Protestant Ethic and the Spirit of Capitalism, London ; Boston: Unwin Hyman (translated: Parsons, T. and Giddens, A., 1930).

Wicksell, K. (1896), A New Principle of Just Taxation, in: Musgrave, R. and Peacock, A., editors, Classics in the Theory of Public Finance, New York: Macmillan, 1958, 72–118.

Wigger, B. U. (2004), On the Intergenerational Incidence of Wage and Consumption Taxes, *Journal of Public Economic Theory*, 6 (1), 1–23.

Winer, S. and Hettich, W. (2002), The Political Economy of Taxation: Positive and Normative Analysis when Collective Choice Matters, Carleton University, Department of Economics – Carleton Economic Papers.

Yaari, M. (1965), Uncertain Lifetime, Life Insurance and the Theory of the Consumer, *Review of Economic Studies*, 32, 137–150.

Yitzhaki, S. and Slemrod, J. (1991), Welfare Dominance: An Application to Commodity Taxation, *The American Economic Review*, 81 (3), 480–496.

Zou, H. (1994), 'The Spirit of Capitalism' and Long-Run Growth, *European Journal of Political Economy*, 10 (2), 279–293.

FSC
www.fsc.org
MIX
Papier aus verantwortungsvollen Quellen
Paper from responsible sources
FSC® C105338

If you have any concerns about our products, you can contact us on
ProductSafety@springernature.com

In case Publisher is established outside the EU, the EU authorized representative is:
Springer Nature Customer Service Center GmbH
Europaplatz 3, 69115 Heidelberg, Germany

Printed by Libri Plureos GmbH
in Hamburg, Germany